der

Mystery

**Famous Unsolved** cides

# Baffling Murder Mysteries
## Famous Unsolved Homicides

*by Marilyn Morgan*

Loompanics Unlimited
Port Townsend, Washington

*Neither the author nor the publisher assumes any responsibility for the use or misuse of information contained in this book. It is sold for entertainment purposes only. Be Warned!*

**Baffling Murder Mysteries**
Famous Unsolved Homicides
© 2001 by Marilyn Morgan

**Published by:**
Loompanics Unlimited
PO Box 1197
Port Townsend, WA 98368
Loompanics Unlimited is a division of Loompanics Enterprises, Inc.
Phone: 360-385-2230
E-mail: service@loompanics.com
Web site: www.loompanics.com

Cover art by Craig Howell

**ISBN 1-55950-213-4**
**Library of Congress Card Catalog Number 2001086813**

# Contents

# Acknowledgements

Writing a book can sometimes feel like an insurmountable undertaking. I'd like to thank the many people who helped me tackle this project.

For their expertise and guidance, Captain T. Michael Nault, Retired, King County Police, Sheriff David Reichert, and Fae Brooks, Chief of the Major Crimes Unit of the King County Sheriff's office. Also thanks to historians Bruce Long, and Jim Nolte, and Seattle Police Department Detective Steve O'Leary.

To author Gregg Olsen for taking the time out of his busy schedule to always allow me to pick his brain and to interview him. Thanks.

To Detective Tom Jenkins of the King County Sheriff's and Cold Case Detectives Rick Ninomiya and Greg Mixsel of the Seattle Police Department for their time and interview, and to all the other police officers who helped me with the research of this book.

Also, to all the librarians at the Seattle and Shoreline public libraries, research libraries at the various newspaper offices, and photo editors who helped me with my sometimes complex research.

# About the Author

Marilyn Morgan is an investigative author who lives in Seattle, Washington.

1

# Introduction

What is it about unsolved murders that stimulates the imagination and sparks the interests of people? And with some cases — the fascination endures through time. The mystery surrounding cases such as Jack the Ripper still spawns endless debates despite the fact that the crimes occurred more than 100 years ago. Movies, books and thousands of newspaper articles are still devoted to the elusive killer. The more unsolvable the crime, the more interest it holds for some of us. Take the case of six-year-old JonBenet Ramsey: hours and hours of television coverage and tons of newspapers and magazine articles are still dedicated to her unsolved murder, and the search and the interest continue.

Okay, I'll admit it — I have always been fascinated by crime. I'm still glued to my television set when an episode of the old television series *Columbo* is on. Before you start to think that I'm ghoulish, it's not the gory details that intrigue me, but it's the art of putting all the facts together and finding out who did it. I guess that's why I always liked *Columbo,* because the show was committed to the deduction part of the crime. We always knew who the killer was right up front, but Lt. Columbo led us down the arduous path of tracking the killer down and discovering the reasons behind the murders. So it seemed inevitable that one day I would write a book about some of the most fascinating unsolved murders of our time.

Of course, there are thousands of unsolved murder cases. Perhaps one day I'll do another volume, but for this book I've selected cases that I think will intrigue and interest you. Some of the cases involve famous people. For example what really happened the night Superman George Reeves died? But I also wanted to include cases that didn't necessarily include famous people — like Ken McElroy. He was a bully who was killed in broad daylight in the middle of town in front of more than forty people who all said they didn't witness anything. Two things they all agreed upon were that they didn't like McElroy and weren't sorry that he was dead.

Since the crimes recounted in this book have so far gone unsolved, I was also interested in theories on who may have been the murderer. Toward that end, I've asked the opinions of historians and police experts to give their opinion on who the likely murderer was in some of these cases.

In the case of the Green River killings, where many young women were randomly murdered in the Seattle, Washington, area, I interviewed detectives who had a prominent role in investigating the serial killing case and their theory on why the killer was never brought to justice.

Why are we so intrigued by crime? I asked my old friend, true crime writer Gregg Olsen, to share his thoughts on what is it about crime that intrigues us, and what keeps us hooked.

So be prepared to be enthralled, and enjoy reading about the cases.

# Chapter One
# The Death of
# William Desmond Taylor

*William Desmond Taylor*

Hollywood may be a hard town to shock — but the murder of popular director William Desmond Taylor proved to be the exception. The murder horrified the town and sent Hollywood into a tailspin. The case still spawns endless debate and speculation on who Taylor's killer might be, and why the case has never been solved.

Taylor was shot in his study at his upscale bungalow in Los Angeles on February 1, 1922. Alvarado Court, the neighborhood where Taylor's bungalow was located, was also home to many others in the movie business, including actor Douglas MacLean and his wife Faith, who lived next door to Taylor.

Hollywood is a town that sells fantasy, and in the movie business, fantasy is much more important than reality. But in 1922, it was also a town besieged by scandals. The stars' real lives didn't reflect the image and fantasy that the town was trying to sell — and the public was finding out. Stories of rampant drug use and sexual promiscuity were making the headlines, and the town was panicked. Several organizations, including women's groups and those concerned with public morality, were warning that Hollywood needed to clean up its act, or there would be consequences to pay. It was during this time that studios began putting moral clauses in the stars' contracts.

In that atmosphere, William Desmond Taylor stood out as the exception. He was intelligent, cultured, reserved, and dignified. More importantly, he lived a life that appeared to be beyond reproach. If he had any demons, they were discretely hidden.

Taylor was president of the Motion Picture Directors Association and was one of the chief executives at Paramount studios, as well as being an active director. At forty-nine, his life appeared ideal. His career was thriving, and he was friends with some of the biggest stars of the day, including

Mary Pickford and Douglas Fairbanks. He was a highly regarded director, and well-respected in the industry.

## What Happened That Night?

On the morning of February 2, 1922, Taylor's cook and valet, Henry Peavey, arrived for work at 7:30 a.m. As he walked up to the house from the driveway, Peavey noticed that the lights were on. He thought that was unusual, since it was a bright, sunny morning, typical for Los Angeles.

When Peavey walked inside, the sight of William Desmond Taylor greeted him, still in the clothes that Peavey had seen him in the night before. Taylor was lying on the floor, on his back near his writing desk. Peavey approached and shook his boss gently before the realization hit him and once it did, he ran from the house, screaming, "Mr. Taylor's dead — Help! Help!"

The neighbors, upon hearing the anguished screams of Peavey, rushed out to see what was happening. They saw the black man running around the courtyard, yelling for help. The scene became chaotic. The manager of Alvarado Court rushed inside, realized that Taylor was dead, and called the police. Meanwhile Taylor's chauffeur had arrived to drive him to work. Thinking quickly, "the chauffeur" instead called Paramount Studios and told them what had happened.

In those days, any hint of scandal, such as the murder of a major studio director, could have destroyed a studio's reputation — which in turn could have derailed projects and could have resulted in millions of dollars in losses. At the time, the film industry produced more than fifteen new movies a week. It wasn't unheard of for actors of the time to make thirty or forty movies a year. The public was hooked on movies, and they wanted their stars angelic.

Someone from the studio immediately called a Paramount executive who lived nearby. He arrived before the police did, and, with the help of some others, effectively "cleaned up" the scene, probably destroying vital evidence in the process. They removed letters, other personal papers, and liquor. It was the Prohibition Era, and people of Taylor's status and wealth often kept an ample supply of liquor in their homes. There were reports that Mabel Normand was also there, and that she reportedly removed letters and other papers.

*Miss Mabel Normand*

When Detective Tom Ziegler of the Los Angeles Police Department arrived, the scene that greeted him was a police officer's nightmare. He was dismayed to see that a crowd had gathered inside the director's bungalow. Henry Peavey was frantically dusting and trying to keep the place clean (probably destroying fingerprints and other evidence). The investigation was complicated even more when a doctor, who was passing by, came in, and upon a cursory examination, told Ziegler that Taylor had died of natural causes due to a stomach hemorrhage. That made sense to some of the neighbors who had gathered, because Taylor was known to have stomach problems. Peavey confirmed the aliment, saying that he often brought his boss medicine for his stomach. Ziegler incorrectly assumed that Taylor had died of natural causes, and allowed more studio people to come in and retrieve more papers.

Approximately two hours later, the Los Angeles Coroner William MacDonald, arrived. When he tried to examine Taylor's body, rigor mortis had set in and the body was stiff and cumbersome. MacDonald had trouble moving the body, and he asked for help. When he and the others turned Taylor over, they saw a pool of blood. MacDonald realized that in all likelihood they were dealing with a murder. Upon further examination, MacDonald discovered a bullet wound in Taylor's back.

On the evening of February 1, Faith MacLean was sitting in her living room. Around 7:45 p.m., she thought she heard a gunshot. She went to look out her door, and in the dim light of the courtyard she saw the shadowy figure of a man — or she thought it was a man. The door to Taylor's bungalow was open and the lights were on. MacLean told police she thought that she heard the man talking to Taylor before the door was closed. She described the man as weighing about 170 pounds, about 5′10″, and said he was young — about twenty-six or twenty-seven years old. She said he had on a dark coat with the collar pulled up, and that he also wore a scarf and a cap. She said she couldn't make out his features, but he turned towards her and smiled, then turned and walked away. She said he didn't rush, or run, or hurry in any way. She thought nothing of it, assumed what she had heard was a car backfiring, and went back to her evening.

## Who was Taylor?

Taylor was a handsome man whom men liked and women loved — apparently as we shall see, one woman who wasn't really a woman yet. She was Mary Miles Minter — the nineteen-year-old starlet who had appeared in many of Taylor's films, and was apparently hopelessly in love (or lust) with the forty-nine-year-old Taylor — a man thirty years her senior.

Taylor was born on April 26, 1872, as William Cunningham Deane Tanner. He was born into a prestigious family in Ireland. He was well-educated not only in arts and culture, but also in manners. As a young man, Taylor was extremely adventurous. He ran away from home when he was eighteen years old, and had developed a curiosity about a lot of things, including the theater. He joined a theater group in England; however his father didn't think being an actor was a suitable profession for someone of his son's background. He sent Taylor to America, hoping that would give his son some direction and a chance to grow into being more of a gentleman. Taylor spent his first few years in America living on a farm doing a variety of odd jobs.

In 1895, Taylor made his way to New York, where he was drawn to acting again. He joined another acting company, and it was there that he met his future wife, Effie Hamilton.

They got married in 1901, and had a daughter named Ethel in 1902. Taylor then left the stage and settled into his life as husband and father. He went into business as an antique dealer. However, suburban life proved to be truly boring for Taylor. He had begun to drink heavily and finally, in 1908, he surreptitiously dissolved his antique business and left his wife, child, and New York.

Tanner changed his name to William Desmond Taylor and resumed his quest for adventure. Taylor traveled and, in 1912, at the urging of some friends, he moved to Hollywood. He had continued to act during his years on the road.

He started acting and appeared in a number of films. One of his most popular movies was *Captain Alvarez*. Even though he loved acting, Taylor found that directing was even more of a challenge for him. He was a popular director with both actors and the studio executives. Hollywood was under siege by women and religious groups who viewed the town as "sin city," and who claimed that Hollywood's films glorified sex and violence. Some of the films of the 1920s were surprisingly risqué, and these groups insisted that the studios tone down the vulgarity and explicit sexuality in their films.

In that climate, Taylor was exactly what the studio needed. He brought artistry and class to the film industry and convinced the studio to produce such literary classics as *Tom Sawyer* and *Anne of Green Gables*.

In 1916, he began working for Paramount Studios, where he directed some of the biggest stars of the time, including Mary Pickford. However, in 1918, when World War I started, Taylor enlisted with the British Army. Partly due to his leadership skills and partly due to his natural intelligence, he became an officer. He returned to Hollywood in 1919, and Paramount enthusiastically welcomed him back.

## Who are the Major Suspects?

MARY MILES MINTER

*Mary Miles Minter*

When Taylor returned to Hollywood, he discovered that a young star was on the horizon. Mary Miles Minter was a blonde nineteen-year-old who projected innocence, charm, and virginal beauty — qualities that were so popular with moviegoers at that time. But as the old saying goes, things are rarely what they seem to be. Mary was hardly virginal; in fact she was sexually active at fifteen, when she engaged in a mock wedding ceremony with a fellow actor, and the two consummated their relationship that night. She would prove to be a great deal of trouble for Taylor.

However, she was a valuable commodity, and became even more so when one of Paramount's biggest stars, Mary Pickford, had left to work for another studio. Mary Miles Minter had stepped up to fill the void. The studio was happy with her work, and did whatever they could to foster her virtuous image.

Mary's manager was her mother Charlotte Minter Shelby. Shelby was probably the original negative prototype of a stage mother. Shelby had tried to become an actress with no success — she had wanted fame, but it never happened for her, and she was determined that fame wasn't going to elude her daughter. Mary and her sister Margaret lived with their mother. Shelby pushed both daughters' careers relentlessly. It soon became apparent that Mary had the talent and the "look" that Hollywood loved, so Margaret was pushed aside. Mary appeared on the New York stage as a child, but Shelby decided that Hollywood was the land of filmmaking and wanted Mary to have a wider audience, so the family headed west. At the age of fourteen, Minter got her very first movie role. To Shelby's credit, after being under contract with Paramount for only two years, she snagged her daughter a six-figure contract. As her manager, Shelby was firmly in control of her daughter, her daughter's career, and her daughter's money. Having achieved the wealth and fame she always desired, Shelby wasn't going to let anyone come between her daughter and herself.

*Charlotte Shelby*

Toward that end, part of Shelby's control consisted of limiting Mary's contact with the outside world, especially men. Of course, Mary had different ideas and she was ripe for romance. At fifteen she "married" actor James Kirkwood, age thirty-five, in a mock wedding ceremony. When they consummated their marriage, it resulted in a pregnancy. When

Shelby found out she was furious, and threatened to kill Kirkwood. Fortunately for Kirkwood, he had returned to England, and Shelby arranged for an abortion for her daughter. From then on, she vowed to keep very tight reins on her daughter.

Mary's heart mended quite fast and when the cultured, sophisticated Taylor directed her in *Anne of Green Gables*, she fell madly in love. She pursued Taylor with enthusiasm, followed him around the studio, and constantly called him at work and at home. She even showed up at his home on occasion, and wrote him embarrassing love letters. By today's standards, her behavior would surely be viewed as stalking. By all accounts, Taylor was a true gentleman and did not take advantage of the young girl's feelings for him — he tried to offer his friendship instead.

Charlotte Shelby was doubtful of Taylor's gentlemanliness. She watched them carefully, and from that time forth she developed a hatred for Taylor. She was convinced that Taylor was interested in her daughter.

Taylor was probably relieved when the movie was completed. However, Mary was in love, or so she thought, and didn't give up her chase. Mary continued to pursue Taylor by writing him love letters and showing up unannounced at his home, literally throwing herself at him.

Shelby held Taylor solely responsible for her daughter's actions. Reports indicate that there were several confrontations at Paramount, usually ending with Shelby shouting that she was going to kill Taylor. Shelby owned a .38-caliber gun — the same caliber that killed Taylor. In another incident, Shelby was furious when her daughter was late coming home. Believing Mary was with Taylor, Shelby went to his home at Alvarado Court with the gun. She demanded to see Mary, telling him if Mary was there she was going to kill

---

him. Taylor denied that Mary was there, and insisted that she search the house. Shelby did search the house, but left when she discovered that her daughter wasn't there.

Despite Shelby's feelings toward Taylor, she allowed Mary to work with him in four more films.

## Mystery Men

While Henry Peavey was never a viable suspect, his predecessor was. Edward Sands was known to have robbed Taylor's home twice. Taylor had reported to the police that Sands had robbed him of several items, including jewels, clothing and a car. Taylor's house was also burglarized twice.

If it was Sands — why did he return to the scene of his crimes? There is speculation that Sands was blackmailing Taylor, or wanted to. Taylor's checkbook was found on his desk the morning after his murder. When detectives examined it closely, they discovered that he had been withdrawing large amounts of money. Taylor lived a rather simple life, so it seemed strange that he would need such large amounts of cash on hand.

From all accounts, Taylor led a quiet life. He had managed to avoid the many scandals that were plaguing Hollywood at the time. Detectives thought that maybe there were secrets in Taylor's life that would make him susceptible to blackmail. They wanted to know more about Edward Sands.

Edward Sands had been hired as Taylor's "Man Friday." Unknown to Taylor, Sands had a shady past. Sands had been charged with embezzlement while serving in the U.S. Navy, which resulted in his dishonorable discharge. He joined the Navy again under an assumed name, but deserted. He joined the U.S. Army under another assumed name, but deserted again. He bounced around the country doing odd jobs before landing in Los Angeles. He started working at Paramount Studios as a cook in the commissary. That's where he met the director and ingratiated himself into Taylor's good graces.

In 1921, Taylor left the country for a few weeks and had invited a friend to stay at his bungalow. Taylor told Sands to look after him and left a blank check. Sands filled in a $5000 amount and cashed it for himself, forged and cashed several other checks, stole jewelry, clothes, and Taylor's car — which police later found wrecked and abandoned.

Evidently, Sands wasn't finished with his old boss. Taylor came home a few months later to discover the back door of the bungalow open, the place ransacked, and jewelry missing. Sands had either thoroughly gone through Taylor's private papers, or knew him before he changed his name, because a few weeks later he sent Taylor tickets to a pawn shop for some of the stolen items in the name of William C. Deane Tanner (Taylor's birth name).

If Sands found out Taylor's original name, he may have also found out other things that would have made Taylor vulnerable to blackmail. Could the man who appeared to have an upstanding life have a secret so bad that he could be blackmailed?

According to an A&E *Biography*, Taylor was gay, and in Hollywood in 1922, being gay was the ultimate scandal. Taylor's career and reputation would have been ruined if the information was true and was revealed. Sadly, being gay was so frowned upon in the 1920s that Paramount's reputation could also have been in jeopardy if it was disclosed that they had hired a gay man. In fact, many believe that on the morning that Taylor was discovered dead, the studio people were not only removing evidence, but planting evidence as well to discourage anyone from thinking that Taylor was gay. The women's panties and pictures are said to have been planted by the studio people.

Another suspect that police pursued was a mysterious stranger, a man who had reportedly asked for directions to Taylor's home. Some think it was a soldier who Taylor had served with, and against whom Taylor had initiated court martial proceedings. Taylor had expressed to some friends once, while walking down the street, that he thought he saw the man. The friends said that Taylor thought the man was dangerous and would have a grudge against him.

One of Taylor's dearest friends could also have been trouble for him. Mabel Normand was one of Hollywood's leading comediennes. She starred in many films with one of the top comedians of the time, Fatty Arbuckle. Normand and Taylor were good friends and shared many interests, including a love of good literature, sometimes spending hours discussing books they had read. A deep and warm friendship developed between them.

There were rumors that the two were having an affair, but it was more likely that they were just close friends.

But the actress who made thousands laugh was a very troubled woman in her personal life. While Taylor enjoyed the reputation of being a gentleman, Normand had no such reputation as a lady. She was a heavy drinker, sexually promiscuous, and abused drugs to the point of addiction, particularly cocaine. Before Taylor's tragic murder, Normand's excesses weren't generally known. During that time, the studio was there to protect her from bad publicity and to clean up her problems. There were whole departments at studios devoted to taking care of stars' problems, whether it was handling the press or the police — they usually managed to protect the stars' reputations.

But Taylor cared about Normand, and he was determined to save her from her addiction. He helped her several times enter drug rehabilitation programs. Normand would relapse back into her cocaine habit and Taylor would help her again. Taylor was a strong drug opponent and Normand's struggle only strengthened his resolve to clean up the drug problem in Hollywood. Taylor became a strong vocal opponent of drug dealers — impeding their efforts to peddle their drugs on the Paramount lot.

He spent the last hour or so of his life with Mable Normand. Had she relapsed once again and lashed out at Taylor? Were drug dealers angry at Taylor for his efforts to rid Hollywood of drugs and take away Normand, one of their best customers?

## The Investigation

An A&E *Biography* about Taylor's life stated that the day Taylor was murdered started out normally. He spent the morning at his office at the studio, left work around 4:00 p.m., and went to a bookstore to pick up a few books that he thought Mabel Normand would enjoy. When he got home he called Normand's home, left a message telling her about the books and asking her to stop by. He arrived back home between 5:30 and 6:30 p.m.

Peavey said that he served Taylor dinner shortly after he arrived home for the evening. A little before 7:00 p.m. Normand arrived while Taylor was on the telephone with a friend. She had brought two bags of peanuts, one for her and one for Taylor. The bag of peanuts that she brought for Taylor was still on the piano the next morning. They talked, and Peavey said he left after serving them cocktails. Peavey told police that he left between 7:15 and 7:20 p.m.

Normand told police that she and Taylor had a pleasant visit, mostly talking about the books that he had purchased for her. She said she left around 7:40 p.m. and that Taylor had walked her to her car. She said they kidded around and shared a laugh, and as she drove away she watched him return to his bungalow.

However, Henry Peavey's statement to the police painted a different view of the visit. He said the two were arguing when he left. He said he didn't hear what the argument was about, but sources of ongoing tension between the two resulted from Normand's continued drug use and Taylor's disapproval in her choices in men.

The police almost immediately ruled out the possibility of robbery. Taylor's expensive watch and a significant amount of cash were found on his body. They suspected blackmail because of the large withdrawals from his bank account. But why? Unfortunately, the studio's attempt to protect Taylor's reputation seriously compromised the investigation into his murder.

Because of Mabel Normand's connection to drugs and Taylor's vocal opposition, police checked out the possibility that drug dealers were involved. Drugs were an important commodity in Hollywood. One theory bandied about in the newspapers was that drug lords had hired a professional killer. That theory didn't pan out, so the police focused on people in Taylor's life.

## What They Found

There were powder burns on Taylor's clothing, suggesting that he was standing very close to the killer when he was shot. According to a *History* channel special on Taylor's death, an expert said that the trajectory of the bullet hole indicated that Taylor was standing facing the shooter, possibly with his arms raised, suggesting that he might have been hugging someone, or maybe he was holding up his arms as if someone was making a threatening gesture. The expert said the bullet trajectory also suggested that the shooter was shorter than Taylor.

Police also found a pink, silk nightgown in one of Taylor's drawers. It obviously belonged to a woman. Initial newspaper reports said the gown had the initials MMM — obviously the initials of Mary Miles Minter. But that was a false report. The gown had no initials. They also found women's panties and allegedly pornographic pictures of women.

Three strands of blonde hair were found on Taylor's jacket. Supposedly, when police compared the hairs to those of hairs found in a brush belonging to Minter, it was a perfect match.

The police found cigarette butts in the area in the back between the MacLeans' and Taylor's bungalows. They thought it was possible that someone was there waiting and watching Taylor. Taylor loved the fresh air and it was his common practice to leave his front door open to enjoy the breeze, sometimes well into the night. One of their theories was that someone was stalking Taylor, waiting for the precise moment that Mable Normand left to make his or her move, and walk freely in the open door.

# Press Out of Control

Fantasy may have been what Hollywood was selling, but scandal is what sells newspapers, and Taylor's death was a scandal made in heaven, whether it had to be manufactured or not. For a man who always tried to live a life of dignity and grace, in death his name was dragged through the mud and he was accused of almost every indecency known to mankind. According to the *History* channel special on Taylor, the press was literally out of control, resulting in a feeding frenzy, with the reporting being largely inaccurate. William Randolph Hearst's newspapers were at the forefront of the inaccurate reporting.

Even though Taylor, by all accounts, had rebuffed the advances of young starlets, particularly Mary Miles Minter, newspapers portrayed Taylor as a man who seduced young women at wild sex parties, having sex with them and then discarding them at his will. The gown that was found at his bungalow the morning of his death was the basis of the newspapers' stories of him having an affair with the screen's virginal beauty, Mary Miles Minter. The story was fueled even further when the press secured a letter from Minter to Taylor professing her unbridled love for him.

The stories didn't stop there; there were also stories accusing Taylor of belonging to homosexual clubs and engaging in homosexual affairs. It was the 1920s, and studios carefully hid the truth of their stars being gay. Additional stories also accused Taylor of not only using heroin and cocaine, but also of being a supplier to actors, most notably Mabel Normand.

The stories seemed designed to compete with, if not compare Taylor with, the stories about the other major scandal of the time, the case of Roscoe "Fatty" Arbuckle. A year earlier, Arbuckle had been charged with the rape and subsequent death of twenty-five-year-old Virginia Rappe (a minor actress who had attended one of Arbuckle's parties). Arbuckle was a brilliant comedian on screen and had a flourishing career. He had netted a one million-dollar-a-year deal with Paramount Studios (which was an astonishing amount in those days). According to a *Court TV* special, Arbuckle was the most popular comedian of his time. He was more popular than Charlie Chaplin or Buster Keaton, who were his contemporaries.

Arbuckle worked hard (he reportedly had made forty-two films in one year) and he played hard. He threw wild parties that consisted of plenty of liquor (despite Prohibition) and plenty of women. Over the Memorial Day weekend in 1921, Arbuckle and a few friends headed to San Francisco's St. Francis Hotel for a party. Arbuckle had finished three films in a row, and wanted some time to relax and have fun.

Virginia Rappe, like many young, pretty women, had tried to start a career in the movie business, but she had virtually no success. With very little talent, Rappe apparently made her reputation in the business in another way. She had allegedly been fired from Keystone Studios for being so promiscuous that she had spread venereal diseases throughout the male population of the studio. At the time of her death she had gonorrhea. It was widely reported that Arbuckle had lured the woman into a bedroom. He weighed 266 pounds and was accused of crushing Rappe by the sheer force of his weight while raping her — causing her bladder to rupture. The press accounts were gruesomely graphic and severely inaccurate with stories of how Arbuckle had torn off the woman's clothes and viciously raped her first with himself and then a wine bottle or a sharp piece of glass. Arbuckle endured three trials between 1921 and 1922. Two of the trials resulted in mistrials, and he was acquitted on the third trial.

Arbuckle's account (which was corroborated by several witnesses) was that he found the woman in the bathroom in pain and vomiting in the toilet. He helped her to his bed in the next room, thinking she had had too much to drink and just needed to rest. When she cried out in pain, the other guests tried to help. They put her in a bathtub full of cold water, hoping to relieve her pain. When she continued to cry out in pain, Arbuckle first called the manager of the hotel, and eventually, a doctor was called. Three days later she was taken to a hospital where she died the next day. The hospital noted the cause of death as peritonitis due to the bladder rupturing.

In reality, it was later revealed that Rappe had had multiple abortions. Later reports indicated that she probably died of a botched abortion that brought on the peritonitis.

The press had portrayed Arbuckle as an abusive brute that had forced himself on an innocent woman. Women's groups were quoted as saying that no woman was safe with this brute on the streets. Even though he was acquitted, the negative press had taken its toll. The public had turned against him and his career was over. Studios were afraid that the scandal and details of Arbuckle's excessive lifestyle were too unpleasant for movie audiences' taste, and he disappeared from the screen for the next ten years. Unfortunately, Arbuckle was never able to stage a comeback. After ten years Paramount did offer Arbuckle a contract, but after signing, Arbuckle died that very night from a heart attack.

Unfortunately for Arbuckle, the facts of his case had little to do with the press coverage — just as the facts had little to do with the press coverage of Taylor's death.

## Charlotte Shelby as a Suspect

The studio tried (mostly in vain) to counteract the attacks on Taylor's character by releasing their own stories of his fight against drug use and his sterling reputation. However, it was years before true accounts of Taylor's reputation were revealed.

The one thing that is certain about the Taylor case is that the investigation was terribly botched from start to finish. From Detective Ziegler not controlling the crime scene the very first day to the initial district attorney, Thomas Lee Woolvine, a friend of Charlotte Shelby's, never asking her for a statement, even though evidence pointed to her as a viable suspect.

The case remained active for fifteen years. When Woolvine died in 1925, the next district attorney, Asa Keyes, did interview Shelby. However, time had passed, evidence had been lost or misplaced (the gown had disappeared along with the strands of hair), and Shelby had an alibi.

Shelby told him that she and her friend Carl Stockdale, an actor, had spent the evening together. She said they were together from 7:00 p.m. to approximately 9:00 p.m. Shelby said she was unaware of Taylor's death until the next day when Stockdale called to inform her of the news around mid-morning. She continued by saying that she then called her chauffeur to drive her to her mother's house, where Mary was staying. Shelby said it was there that she told her daughter of Taylor's death. Mary was so overwhelmed with grief that she rushed to Taylor's home and cried inconsolably.

Shelby told the District Attorney that she had owned a .38-caliber revolver (the type of gun that killed Taylor). She said she had asked her chauffeur to dispose of the bullets from the gun in 1920 after her daughter, Mary, had used the gun in a failed suicide attempt. Keyes concluded that the evidence against Shelby was not strong enough to pursue charges.

The case remained dormant until a new district attorney, Burton Fitts, took office in 1929. Fitts interviewed Shelby's chauffeur Chaucey Eaton, who told a different account. He said that Shelby had called him over around 7:00 a.m. the day that Taylor was killed. Eaton told the D.A. that when he arrived Shelby told him that Taylor had been murdered and he drove her to her mother's to see Mary. (Peavey didn't find Taylor until 7:30 a.m., and because of the confusion at his home that morning, it took some time to conclude that Taylor had been murdered.)

There is a great deal of debate as to why Shelby wasn't arrested or viewed as a stronger suspect in the early days of the investigation into Taylor's death. There is speculation that both Woolvine and Keyes had subverted evidence against Shelby (the hair strands and nightgown were not found during later investigations), and she in turn had paid them off.

According to the *History* channel, Shelby claimed in a lawsuit against her broker in later years that he had embezzled almost a half-million dollars from her. However, the broker claimed that Shelby had told him to use that money as payoffs to Woolvine, Keyes, and Carl Stockdale, the man who coincidentally had provided her with an alibi the night that Taylor was murdered. Nothing came of the allegations.

Shelby's other daughter, Margaret Fillmore, also made a startling claim against her mother. In 1937, in a lawsuit she filed against her mother, she stated publicly that she thought her mother had killed Taylor. She had no evidence to back up her claim. It was clear that Margaret hated her mother — the two had been at odds for years. The tension between the two resulted from Shelby lavishing all of her attention on

Mary, and the fact that Margaret had battled alcoholism for years. At one point Shelby had Margaret institutionalized. Margaret died a couple of years later from complications due to alcoholism.

With everyone from her own daughter to Taylor's friends to some members of the press accusing her of killing Taylor, Shelby decided that she had had enough. Fifteen years after Taylor was murdered she demanded a grand jury investigation to clear her name. The old saying, "Be careful what you wish for, because you just might get it," certainly held true, because the District Attorney granted Shelby her wish.

Several witnesses were called, and some interesting bits of information emerged from that grand jury investigation.

Shelby's former secretary said that she had heard Shelby make repeated threats against Taylor's life. She also said that Shelby was worried about a rumor she had heard about Mary and Taylor eloping (a situation that was highly unlikely).

Shelby's daughter Margaret testified that her mother had kept her sister, Mary, locked in her room the day that Taylor was murdered. She said Mary had escaped from the room and returned later that evening, very upset.

The former chauffeur said that after Taylor's murder, Shelby did in fact give him the pistol and told him to dispose of the bullets. The gun was a .38-caliber. He testified that Shelby had said she was afraid that Mary would use the gun to commit suicide. He hid the bullets in the basement of Shelby's home without her knowledge, and returned the gun to her. Sure enough, even though it was fifteen years later, when investigators checked on his testimony they found the bullets. Tests revealed that the bullets were the same size and weight as the bullet that was removed from Taylor's body. However, without the gun it wasn't possible to check the ri-

---

fling marks, therefore, legally, the connection to Shelby's gun could not be made.

Shelby explained that she couldn't produce the gun because after Mary tried to commit suicide, she gave the gun to her mother to dispose of and she never saw it again. Margaret confirmed that Shelby did give the gun to her grandmother, not because she was afraid that Mary would use it, but because Shelby was afraid that the police were getting close to discovering the truth. Margaret claimed that her grandmother threw the gun away while on a trip to Louisiana.

The star witness that everyone wanted to see, and the press was clamoring to hear from, was Mary Miles Minter. However, she supported her mother's innocence, saying that her mother had no reason to want Taylor dead. Being a suspect herself at one time, she denied that the gown that was supposedly found at Taylor's was hers. (Some suspected Minter because she may have been upset over his repeated rebuffs of her advances.) She denied there was a gown, letters, or anything else to connect her to Taylor. That was true to an extent, since the gown and the blonde hair sample had mysteriously disappeared.

After hearing all the evidence, the grand jury rendered its verdict. They neither brought an indictment nor did they clear Shelby. The case officially ended in 1938 — with no indictments, no convictions and not even a clear-cut suspect.

## Careers Left in Ruins

William Desmond Taylor was murdered, but many people suffered from the fallout of the investigation into his death.

With the news of her drug addiction and promiscuous life-style on center stage during the initial investigation, Mabel Normand's career all but died. She tried to reconstruct her career, but to no avail. She contracted tuberculosis and died at age thirty-seven in 1930.

At first Mary Miles Minter had said she had not seen Taylor since well before Christmas. But when confronted with both the fact that the hairs on Taylor's jacket matched hers, and a note Minter had written professing her undying love for him (the note read, "Dearest, I love you, I love you, I love you!") Minter confessed to police that she had visited Taylor on January 30 and left the note. She said she stayed for a while and she and Taylor shared some tender moments. After the press accounts of her obsessive pursuit of Taylor and her affairs with other men, she was no longer seen as the innocent, virginal beauty and her film career was over. Even though she made a few more pictures for Paramount after Taylor's murder, audiences boycotted her films and the studio released her from her contract less than a year after Taylor's death. She died of heart failure in 1984.

## What the Expert Says

Bruce Long, author and historian of both silent films and Taylor's life, has devoted hours of research and writings into the death of William Desmond Taylor. He has written what some consider to be the most comprehensive account of Taylor's life and death in his Taylorology series on his website. He spoke to me from his home in Scottsdale, Arizona, to discuss Taylor and his theory on who killed him.

"From all of the research that I've conducted on the Taylor case, I personally think there are two strong suspects," he said. "Maybe the strongest being Charlotte Shelby. There is evidence to believe that if she didn't actually pull the trigger, she at least orchestrated Taylor's murder."

"She was extremely jealous of anyone who Mary became close to and she threatened Taylor many times, demanding that he stay away from Mary," said Long.

Long points out that if Mary had indeed married Taylor, or anyone for that matter, Charlotte Shelby would no longer have control of, or access to, Mary's income. Money and power was very important to Charlotte Shelby. In a way, it made up for her own failure as an actress.

Long said another essential fact is the matching bullet. "When investigators found the bullets from the .38-caliber gun in Shelby's house, the unfired bullets matched the fatal bullet retrieved from Taylor's body," he said. "Shelby was shrewd. By getting rid of the gun, she probably knew that the police couldn't conclusively prove that the bullet came from her gun."

In addition, Long said that Shelby's alibi for the evening, Carl Stockdale, received monthly payments from Shelby. As a matter of fact, when Faith MacLean was later shown a picture of Stockdale, she said it was possible he was the man she had seen leaving Taylor's bungalow the night that he was murdered — but she couldn't be absolutely positive.

Another strong point against Shelby, said Long, was that two separate witnesses, the chauffeur, Chaucey Eaton, and Marjorie Berger, stated that Shelby called them early on February 2, around 7:00-7:30 a.m. saying that Taylor had been shot and murdered. "These conversations took place before Shelby could have possibly known that Taylor was murdered unless she was somehow involved, since Henry Peavey didn't discover the body until around 7:30 that morning," said Long.

"The other person that I strongly suspect is Edward Sands," said Long. "Sands had an extensive criminal background." He explained that because of Sands' years in the service he was very familiar with firearms. Sands even owned a .45-caliber automatic, and although Taylor was killed with a .38, it would be reasonable to assume that someone with Sands' background would know how to obtain another gun.

"In addition, witnesses had placed Sands in Los Angeles a mere two days before Taylor was shot and murdered," said Long.

Long also said that Sands had a familiarity with Taylor and knew his habits (for example, leaving his front door open at night).

"It was obvious that Sands was stalking Taylor because he came back to burglarize Taylor's house at least once — subsequently pawning Taylor's jewelry and mailing him the pawn tickets with a sarcastic note," Long said.

In reality, Charlotte Shelby seemed to have been the only person with any real reason to harm Taylor. In the A&E *Biography* special it was suggested that a possible scenario was that Mary Miles Minter escaped from her mother's that day and headed for Taylor's home. Once there, Taylor tried to offer comfort by embracing her. Shelby either followed her daughter or knew where she was headed, and went to Taylor's. It is speculated that she probably walked in on the innocent scene, confronted Taylor, and when he walked over to explain, she shot him in a fit of rage.

# Chapter Two
# What Happened to
# Judge Joseph Crater?

*Judge Joseph Crater*

On the evening of August 6, 1930, Judge Joseph Crater had dinner with a couple of friends at a popular restaurant on West Forty-Fifth Street in New York. A little before 9:00 p.m., they walked with him out of the restaurant where he hailed a cab. Judge Crater disappeared and was never seen or heard from again. The judge, an avid theatre fan, was on his way to see the hit Broadway show *Dancing Partner* — he had a ticket waiting for him at the box office. He took a cab even though the theatre was only a block away from the restaurant. What is known is that his theatre ticket was picked up, but the box office clerk wasn't sure if it was Judge Crater who picked it up. It's not sure if the Judge actually saw the play, but what is sure is that the Judge was never seen again. His disappearance remains one of the most baffling mysteries of the century. Was he murdered, or did he simply disappear to start a new life? It seems no one knows for sure.

On the surface, Judge Crater appeared to be a respectable justice who had everything going right in his life. He was only forty-one-years-old when President Franklin Roosevelt appointed him to the New York State Supreme Court. This appointment came four months before Crater disappeared.

Judge Crater had attended law school at Columbia University in New York. He had a successful practice long before becoming a judge. He had many interests, but one of his passions was politics. He was savvy and seemed to have made all the right connections for his career. One of those moves was becoming a member of one of the most powerful political organizations in the city — the Tammany Club. Of course, being a member of Tammany could have possibly led to his disappearance.

As was common in those days, a lot of powerful political groups were corrupt. Some members of Tammany were being investigated for various illegal activities including buying judgeships. However, Judge Crater's reputation seemed beyond reproach. There weren't any facts or innuendo that linked him to the corruption.

By most accounts, Judge Crater had further aspirations for his life. His appointment to the State Supreme Court was only temporary. His was completing the term of a judge who had retired. But his friends and colleagues all said that he wanted the job permanently, and was preparing to run for the fourteen-year term position. They said he was looking forward to campaigning and saw the State Supreme Court as a stepping-stone to another goal — the United States Supreme Court.

## Judge Crater's Last Days

Crater and his wife Stella owned a house in Augusta, Maine. It was a nice summer getaway from New York City's heat and hectic lifestyle.

During most of the summer Crater traveled back and forth, while Stella usually stayed in Maine all summer. Crater had planned to spend most of the month of August in Maine and return to the city at the end of the month, when the next session of the court convened.

On August 1, he got a call to return to the city. His wife told police that her husband didn't discuss the call with her — he only said he had to return to the city and that he would return to Maine on August 9 to continue the vacation.

Crater returned to his apartment on Fifth Avenue. He gave the live-in maid the next several days off. It was August 4, and by all accounts during the next few days his life was extremely normal.

According to a *History* channel special he spent most of his days, as usual, working in his chambers. He went to his office the day he disappeared. However, those around him noticed that he was acting strangely. For example, he asked one of his assistants to go to the bank and cash a check for more than $5,000. He wasn't a high roller, so withdrawing that much money raised suspicion. He also took his personal files with him when he left for the day. To the assistant's knowledge, it was the first time that the judge had taken *any* of his personal files home, not to mention the fact that he took them *all* with him. One assistant commented to police that the judge had seemed distracted and worried, but he didn't pry.

Later that evening Crater went to the theatre to get a ticket for that evening's performance of *Dancing Partner*. The theater clerk said he didn't have a ticket at that time, but would get one for the Judge and he could pick it up at the ticket window before curtain call.

Judge Crater then went to Billy Haas' restaurant, a very renowned restaurant in the 1930s. There he ran into an old friend, a lawyer named William Klein. Klein asked Crater to join him and his lady guest for the evening for dinner. The judge did, and Klein told police they had a pleasant evening and that Crater hadn't mentioned any problem that he was worried about. He said the Judge left in a cab around 9:00 p.m. The play started at 8:00 p.m. — making the Judge over an hour late for the performance. Yet, the theatre ticket clerk couldn't say whether it was actually Judge Crater who picked up his ticket. One fact is known — the ticket was picked up. Police also started an active search for the cab who picked up Judge Crater at the restaurant to see if the judge had actually gone to the theatre. They placed ads in newspapers, they made announcements on radio stations, and they put out flyers asking for help — but no cab driver ever came forward. Judge Crater was last seen getting into the cab — and no one has ever seen or heard from him again.

Mysteriously, the judge's disappearance wasn't reported for quite some time. When he didn't return to Maine on August 9, his wife was worried, but didn't try to locate him until a week later. She claimed she constantly called their New York apartment. When there was no answer, all she did was send the chauffeur down to check out the apartment. He found nothing and reported that back to her.

When Judge Crater didn't report for duty when the Court began its session on August 26, his colleagues became concerned. They started asking around but came up empty handed. However, it wasn't until September 3 that the police were notified that Judge Crater had been missing for almost a month.

The police were perplexed as to how a man like Judge Crater could disappear off the face of the earth, and why it took almost a month for anyone to report it. Someone must have noticed the Judge the night he disappeared. A story published by the *New York Times*, describes Crater as an uncommon-looking man. He was "exceptionally tall, had a comparatively small head for a man his height, prominent eyes and broad shoulders that made his neck look long." He was also a minor celebrity in town — meaning that a lot of people knew who he was. In all probability, if he had picked up his ticket at the theatre window, the clerk would have remembered seeing him.

Judge Crater was a complex man whose life seemed full of contradictions. The police turned up some interesting facts in his personal life. Crater apparently had many affairs with showgirls and had a longtime mistress, which may have been why Mrs. Crater didn't report his disappearance right away.

Maybe she was used to him spending time with his mistress.
He also frequented speakeasies, one in particular on a regular
basis. His favorite was allegedly the same one where mobsters such as Dutch Schultz regularly visited. However, his
colleagues had described Crater as a teetotaler who led a
quiet life.

If Crater was taking bribes or payoffs, it didn't show up in
his financial records. The police concluded that his finances
reflected what those of a man of his income should be. Of
course, if Crater had intended to disappear he could have
disposed of any extra income and wouldn't have left a paper
trail.

After an investigation with very little to go on, the police
hardly knew any more about Judge Crater's disappearance
than when they started — he had disappeared without a
trace.

## The Theories

The disappearance of the prominent State Supreme Court
Justice has fueled many theories about what actually happened. Judge Crater did seem to have led, if not a double life,
one that was diametrically opposed to the life most people
thought he led.

One theory was that Judge Crater might have disappeared
voluntarily. He may have set up the situation where he could
disappear and wouldn't be missed for a long while — which
gave him plenty of opportunity to cover his tracks. Newspaper reports indicate that he went to inquire about the theatre
tickets a little after 7:00 p.m. — why then would he go to
dinner when the curtain went up at 8:00 p.m.? By taking

most of his personal papers with him, it would be next to impossible to trace some important aspects of his personal life.

Another theory is that Judge Crater was tired of his empty, predictable life with his wife, and ran off with one of the showgirls with whom he was having an affair. Maybe the Judge did fall in love and didn't want to go through the disgrace of a messy divorce. (In the 1930s, respectable men didn't leave their wives for showgirls.)

Of course, as far as his personal life, the Judge was certainly handling his affairs with discretion. Most people who knew him believed that Judge Crater was ambitious and wanted a shot at becoming a judge for the United States Supreme Court.

If those around Judge Crater were involved with shady dealings, there was no evidence that he had engaged in any illegal or even questionable conduct. He wasn't under investigation and there isn't any evidence that he was under suspicion. However, if he was involved, then maybe he feared the destruction of his career and reputation was imminent.

Of course, most historians discount that theory. Most say that the Judge was indeed murdered — maybe the victim of something as simple as a robbery gone badly. However, his body was never found and, after all, an everyday robber would have no reason to get rid of the Judge's body.

However, historians say the most likely theory is that Judge Crater met with some of the members from Tammany Hall. Perhaps he found out more damaging information and he wanted to confront them. Or perhaps they found out something about him and wanted blackmail money. That would explain him withdrawing a large sum of money. The papers that he took from his office were never found — was someone after those papers?

In an article written in the *New York Times*, a writer who has devoted hours of research to the case says that she thinks Judge Crater had every intention of going to the theatre that night, but someone posing as a cab driver kidnapped him from the restaurant. He was then taken somewhere and killed, she theorizes, to keep him from testifying in the investigation of the sale of judges' seats. That would explain why no cab driver ever came forward.

Five years after Crater disappeared, the police department declared him dead. Even after all these years, interest in the case remains high. In all likelihood, no one will ever solve the mystery surrounding Judge Crater's disappearance.

# Chapter Three
# The Mad Butcher
# of Cleveland

In the annals of unsolved murders, there is none more fascinating than the case of the unsolved serial killings that happened in Cleveland, Ohio, in the 1930s, when twelve people were savagely murdered and mutilated by a man that the press had dubbed "The Mad Butcher." Twelve was the official number of victims credited to the murderer, but most feel the number was even higher.

In his book, *Butcher's Dozen*, John Bartlow Martin describes the killer as "...a master criminal... It can be argued that he was the greatest murderer of all time." Part of the intrigue is that the concept of a serial killer was virtually unheard of in the mid-1930s. Even today, when serial killers have become a modern-day reality, relationships between murders often go unnoticed by the police for a long time, resulting in delays in the classification as serial killings. The police investigated the Cleveland murders by focusing their investigation on family and acquaintances of the victims, at least the victims that were identified. However, we know today that serial killers usually choose strangers as their victims. Using the "family and acquaintance" approach would do little to help in catching the killer. Forensic science wasn't sophisticated in those days, and the most cutting edge

technology was the recent invention of the polygraph machine.

*Eliot Ness*

Another intriguing part of the case was the involvement of Eliot Ness, the legendary leader of the elite law enforcement team dubbed The Untouchables. Ness, who was widely credited with fighting racketeering, police corruption, and making the case against Al Capone that sent him to jail, had become the Safety Director for the city of Cleveland. Cleveland was the seventh largest city in the country and, like Chicago, the Cleveland police department at the time was rapidly becoming one of the most corrupt in the country. Drawing on his knowledge of criminology (he had a Master's degree), Ness' goal was to turn the Cleveland police department into a well-respected, efficient and professionally run organization.

In his book, *Torso,* Steven Nickel described Cleveland, at that time, as a city very much in "contrast" with itself. The city could be divided literally into two sections. One was the vibrant side of the city that had experienced a great deal of resurgence coming out of the Depression and was attracting businesses and prestigious conventions to town, such as the Republican National Convention. The other side was definitely the forgotten section and home to those hit hardest by the Depression — the city's poorest, homeless, hobos, and shanty houses distinguished this area. These people sought refuge along the Kingsbury Run River. Nickel describes the river as more of a gully than a river, one that was dark, dank and made it easy to blend into obscurity.

It all started on the afternoon of September 23, 1935, when two young boys running through an open field after school made a grisly discovery — the body of a man with no head. When the Cleveland police arrived, they discovered not only one body, but another man's body only a few feet away. Both bodies had been decapitated. Both bodies were naked, and their penises had been removed. After searching, they found the heads of both men. The coroner's report indicated that both men had been murdered by decapitation — an unusual and messy way of committing murder. The coroner also reported that the younger man had deep rope burns on his wrists, indicating that the victim was conscious at the time of the decapitation.

The first victim was never identified; however, the second victim was identified through his fingerprints as Edward Andrassy, age twenty-eight. The police knew Andrassy as a seedy character, a troublemaker, and a petty criminal who spent most of his time in sleazy bars where he usually picked fights when he was drunk.

According to Steven Nickel's book, *Torso*, there were reports that Andrassy was a pimp for both women and young men, that he dealt in pornography, and that he was a man who liked to have affairs with married women (supposedly one husband had threatened to kill him). It was also rumored that he was a male prostitute and bisexual.

The two men had been murdered at one location and moved to the Kingsbury Run area afterwards. They concluded that the same person killed both men with a sharp blade such as a butcher's knife. The bodies had to have been carried down the deep ravine, because cars couldn't get any closer than 100 feet. Because of that, the police theorized that the killer had to be a very strong man.

The police investigation revealed that Andrassy had left home on Thursday September 19, 1935. He wasn't heard from again. According to the coroner's report, he was killed on Friday night and the schoolboys found his body Monday afternoon. After following up on many dead-end clues, detectives finally put the case on their inactive list.

Even though the city of Cleveland was rebounding from the Depression in 1935, it had other problems. It was a city beset with a spiraling crime rate, mobster influence, prostitution and gambling rings and, especially, police corruption. The newly elected mayor, Harold Burton, had run an old-fashioned law and order campaign and desperately wanted to eliminate corruption and crime in Cleveland. Burton won and true to his word of trying to clean up the city, he recruited and appointed the stalwart against police corruption himself, Mr. "Untouchable" Eliot Ness, as Director of Public Safety. Ness, who was fresh from his "triumphs" as Chicago's tough crime fighter wanted the opportunity, and immediately set about putting programs in place that he promised would eliminate police corruption.

On January 26, 1936, another murder was reported, and police found parts of a woman's body floating along Kingsbury Run. The coroner concluded that the woman's death was due to decapitation, and that she had been dead from two to four days. Coroner Pearse also concluded that, as in the Andrassy case, whoever committed this murder made nearly professional surgical cuts, as if he had expertise in this area.

Again through fingerprints, the police were able to identify the victim as Florence Polillo. Like Andrassy, Polillo had run afoul of the law. She had been arrested many times for prostitution. They also found out that Polillo had a drinking problem and would become belligerent and violent when she was drunk. She had been married twice, but had left her husband both times. Polillo's life degenerated after her failed marriages. She resorted to working as a prostitute to earn money — drugs, heavy drinking, and prostitution had taken their toll on the woman.

When the rest of Polillo's body was found a few weeks later, Coroner Pearse's conclusion was that, as with the first two victims, Polillo had been murdered by decapitation.

And, like the other two murders, what few leads there were led nowhere. Therefore, Polillo's murder investigation was also put on the back burner.

Sergeant James Hogan, one of the primary investigators on the case, didn't believe the cases were connected, one reason being that they had occurred more than four months apart. (Serial killing investigators today know that most of these killers initially engage in a cooling off period between killings.)

The citizens of Cleveland were generally happy with the job that Eliot Ness was doing as safety director. Ness was energetic about implementing his plans for cleaning up the city. In fact, the police department was regaining respectability and organized crime was held in check. The strange murders didn't get much publicity, and hadn't yet seeped into the public's mind.

On Friday, June 5, two boys on their way to fish decided to take a shortcut through Kingsbury Run. The boys spotted a pair of pants and went to investigate. A grotesque discovery terrorized them — a man's head rolled out from the brush. They ran back to one of the boy's houses and, frightened, waited to call the police until the boy's mother came home.

The railroad trains ran parallel to Kingsbury Run and the railroad police station was located in this area, partly to patrol and partly to prevent the hobos from jumping the trains. The next day the police found parts of the rest of the man's body that the boys had discovered near the railroad police station. The police may have thought this was a cruel joke, leaving parts of a body so close to the police station. However, modern day evidence indicates that serial killers often engage in a weird cat-and-mouse game with police. The killers try to taunt the police by leaving subtle or not-so-subtle forms of communication — daring the police to catch them.

This victim was in his mid-twenties and had six nautical tattoos on his body. The police again concluded that the young man was killed somewhere else and his body, or what was left of it, was brought to Kingsbury Run and dumped. The young man was clean-shaven, well-groomed, and obviously not a resident of Kingsbury Run.

Coroner Pearse was surprised and disturbed to find that this man had also died as a result of decapitation and that the killing had the same characteristics as the other murders. Pearse knew that this was the fourth victim who had died by decapitation within a year, and wondered if one person was responsible for the killings. It appeared a pattern was definitely forming. He told Detective David Cowles his concerns. Detective Cowles was the department's forensics expert, and was beginning to think along the same lines as Coroner Pearse. He asked a few of the newspapers to run a photograph of the man's face, hoping someone would recognize him, but no one reported knowing him. Cowles wondered if these murders were related to one that happened in 1934. That year, the bottom half of a woman's torso had been found floating up Kingsbury Run. The upper half of her body had been found a couple of weeks earlier. The woman was never identified and her head was never found. She was only identified as the "Lady of the Lake." (The Lady of the Lake was never officially classified with the other murders.) Stories of the bizarre murders began to appear in the newspapers. Rumors of a demonic killer surfaced.

By the time that June rolled around, city officials were becoming concerned about the killings because they were expecting the biggest convention that the city had ever hosted. The Republican National Convention was due in town on that Monday, June 8, and parts of dead bodies were popping up in the river. The mayor was nervous, and Eliot Ness decided that he needed to, at least, be briefed on the killings. Ness listened as Hogan explained what he knew about the murders.

Hogan didn't believe the murders were related or committed by one person. While the murders were similar, in his opinion they were also very different. He told Ness that the three deaths were similar in that they were placed in an area where they were sure to be found quickly; and, except for the decapitations, the rest of their bodies were intact. However, the body of Florence Polillo was not only decapitated, but dismembered as well.

Ness wanted Hogan and his detectives to handle the cases, because Ness wanted to get back to what he thought was important — fighting corruption. Ness thought that widespread corruption was prevalent at the top levels of the police force. He was determined to restore competency and good morale to the force. One change he made was to transfer more than 100 police officers who headed the local precinct's corruption rings. He demoted officers who were the most glaringly corrupt and promoted officers whom he thought had earned the right to be promoted, but never had been.

Ness' policies were having an impact. Slowly, the police department was regaining its respectability. Mob influence was held in check, and crime was generally down. However, Ness' policies also gained him powerful enemies. One was a politically savvy and controversial state congressman named Martin L. Sweeney. The Congressman thought Ness was more interested in busting hard-working cops who maybe once took a small bribe, as opposed to catching real criminals. He pointed to the city's still-high murder rate as an example.

---

Meanwhile, the police worked diligently, trying to identify the victim with the tattoos, hoping his identification would lead to clues about the killer. Since the man's tattoos were nautical, detectives suspected that he was a sailor. They took the man's picture to various local naval ports and known sailor hangouts, but their efforts didn't result in identification.

The investigative team was getting nowhere, and just when they thought things couldn't get any worse, in July, 1936, another victim was found. A teenage girl discovered the headless body of a man. The police located the head about fifteen feet from the body. Coroner Pearse examined the body which was in an advanced state of decomposition. He determined that death was caused by decapitation, accomplished with the same expertise Pearse had come to associate with the killer. However, there was something new. This was the first victim in the series who was killed in the location where she was found.

After another decapitation murder, Hogan had no choice but to agree with his colleagues that the killer was probably the same person. Ness, who was a person who liked to court the press, wanted to keep this information away from the press in order to avoid panic among the people in the city. Despite Hogan and Ness' efforts, stories of the bizarre murders were prominently featured in the papers on almost a daily basis.

On September 10, another torso was found floating in the Kingsbury Run River. As the police and fire rescue squads scoured the area looking for the rest of the body, the news spread, as a huge crowd gathered to watch. They recovered two legs, the right thigh, a hat with blood spots, and a work shirt that was soaked in blood. The crowd looked on anxiously, at the prospect of their town being in the grip of a mad killer.

Not to anyone's surprise, the coroner concluded that death was caused by decapitation. The press reported that the decapitations were the work of one killer. They even dubbed the murderer "The Mad Butcher."

The mayor didn't like the publicity the murders were receiving, so he had a discrete meeting with Ness. Ness then called a summit of some of the principals on the case, which included Sergeant James Hogan, his newly appointed head of the homicide division; David Cowles, head of the crime lab; Coroner Pearse; the Chief of Police; and one of the pathologists who had performed the autopsies on some of the victims. Ness considered Hogan and Cowles two of the department's brightest officers.

Pearse gave Ness a detailed rundown on the murders, including the information that some of the bodies had been drained of blood and cleaned. The bodies were also soaked with some kind of chemical. Hogan added that the department had conducted a thorough investigation on the initial two victims, but that the investigation had been hampered by the fact that detectives were unable to identify one of the victims because his head and hands had been removed. Hogan explained that, like the tattooed man, these men were killed at one location and carried to Kingsbury Run. Hogan also talked about the Lady of the Lake, and explained that there was little to go on; her head and hands had never been found, and no one had reported a woman around her age missing. The police did not believe that she was part of the current crop of killings.

Ness asked them if they thought the other murders were related. After a lengthy discussion, it turned out that one factor they agreed on was that the killings were probably done

---

by one person. Secondly, they agreed that the decapitations were done by someone with an expertise in human anatomy, maybe even a surgeon. Because of the surgical precision of the decapitations, a lot of the detectives thought that the killer was most likely a doctor. However, Pearse and the pathologist didn't subscribe to that theory, and thought anyone good with a knife, perhaps a butcher or a hunter, were equally good candidates.

They also agreed that the killer was more than likely a strong man, because it takes a great deal of strength to carry out a decapitation, and it also took a great deal of strength to move the bodies to a different area after the killings. In addition, since decapitations take time to carry out, the killer had to be very familiar with the Kingsbury Run area not to be discovered.

It was the 1930s, when even the concept of a serial killer was foreign to police departments, so how to go about solving one was baffling to say the least. Ness agreed with the conclusions that he heard. He thought there were too many similarities for the murders not to be related. Ness wanted Hogan to operate on that premise. But Ness was getting pressure from the mayor, and he instructed those involved with the case not to talk with the media, especially about the theory that there was a single killer on the loose.

Hogan was still skeptical, but since he didn't have another explanation he went along with the theory; whereas, Cowles' every instinct told him that one person was responsible for these crimes. Unfortunately, Hogan and Cowles were unaware of the unique techniques used to investigate serial killings, so they set about investigating the crimes like they would any other murder. They checked out the families, friends, and acquaintances of the victims, looking for any motive or opportunity, unaware that most serial killings are stranger, or very casual acquaintance, killings.

According to an A&E *Biography* special, a straight homicide was not Ness' forte. His lifelong dream, however, was to become known as the best law enforcement officer in the country. Ness thought the way to accomplish that was to eliminate police corruption in the city. He reasoned that the death of a couple of petty criminals couldn't compare to that duty, and therefore gave Hogan complete authority to handle the cases in the best way he saw fit.

However, after the latest murder, the mayor wanted Ness to head the investigation, thinking it would calm the city to know that the safety director was personally taking matters in hand. So, Eliot Ness took a more active approach. He assigned twenty-five detectives to the cases. The detectives were given different assignments. Some combed the missing persons files, others followed up on clues, and others went about interviewing most of the hobos they could find in the Kingsbury Run area. They were feeling pressure from Ness. The public was nervous. A special hotline was set up at the station to take the numerous calls. As with any multi-crime case, citizens became anxious, and hundreds of tips were reported to the police from anyone who thought they knew anything. The detectives diligently followed up on every tip, mostly on direct orders from Ness. Ness wanted these killings solved so that he could get back to what he felt was important — fighting corruption.

It was an arduous task. The detectives thought most of these so-called leads would go nowhere, and they were right. Also, there were many "strange" people in Cleveland at the time. In *Torso*, Nickel describes the questioning of a man who liked to have sex with chickens, and of the voodoo doctor who was previously implicated in a decapitation murder in a separate case. They were all questioned, but most were let go because of insufficient evidence, or in some cases arrested for other crimes, but none could be connected to the murders at Kingsbury Run.

Detectives even tried going undercover as hobos and hanging out in the Kingsbury Run area, keeping an eye on, and questioning anyone they found suspicious. "Butcher's Bait" was how one newspaper described the undercover operation. Some also hung out in gay bars and steam baths — since at least one of the male victims (Andrassy) had reportedly been involved in homosexual relationships with men who had a tendency for violence. The detectives didn't adapt well to their new environment and, naturally, they didn't uncover a lot of information.

After the latest murder, *The Cleveland News* offered a generous reward for any information leading to the killer. The killings were a hot topic — people were fascinated by the grisly murders. It seemed that everyone in the city had a theory of who the killer was, and why he killed. One theory that was constantly bandied about to police was that the killer was a doctor who killed people of lower economic status to rid the world of them. The police took this theory seriously, since it was also a theory they had.

Even though the notion of a serial killer was not well known, one important feature of the Kingsbury Run killings was the posing of the bodies and leaving them in plain sight. Police recognize this today as a signature of a serial killer. Even though Eliot Ness and his detectives didn't recognize the significance of leaving the bodies where they were sure to be found, they knew they were dealing with a unique killer, someone who liked to taunt the police. They reasoned that while he was obviously psychopathic, he was probably not insane. Cowles thought the killer probably worked and mingled in society without suspicion.

## Profiling the Killer

Ness met with experts to try to understand the killer and to discover what motivated him. The experts told him that the killer could not be a woman due to the factor of physical strength — decapitation itself requires a great deal of strength, and at least three of the victims were murdered at one location and literally carried to Kingsbury Run. And while they agreed that the killer had an impressive knowledge of anatomy, there was no particular reason to think the killer was a doctor. This was much the same information that the detectives and others had already told him. Since decapitation is a messy procedure and there was very little blood found at the scene of the bodies, the killer must have had a secluded, quiet place to commit the murders. What they didn't know was why — what was motivating the murderer to kill? Why were his victims petty criminals or people from the lower socioeconomic strata? Today's serial killer experts, such as Captain Michael Nault, say that victims like those in the Kingsbury Run murders and today's frequent victims, prostitutes, are not picked simply because of the killer's desire to rid society of undesirables, but rather because these people are readily available and can be easily lured away with the promise of a few dollars.

Dumping the bodies at Kingsbury Run was also unique to this crime. Out of the murders so far, four bodies were dumped in Kingsbury Run and one almost mockingly close to the railroad police station. It was almost a challenge by the killer — saying to them "you can't catch me."

One well-known detective who had joined the team was Detective Peter Merylo. Merylo was considered a very intelligent man and had a reputation for being tenacious in solving a crime, working sometimes around the clock to follow up on leads. He was the one who conducted the questioning of some of the city's more "eccentric" characters who had fallen under suspicion.

Merylo hated what he termed perversion and he unfortunately thought of gay men as perverts. In the 1930s homosexuality was illegal in Cleveland and Merylo purportedly frequented gay bars, followed men home, and sometimes arrested them. He was convinced that the Kingsbury Run murderer was gay, because a majority of the victims were male and they seemed to him to be sexually motivated. In addition, suspicion fell on both the city's hobo population, most of whom were simply down on their luck, and also the eccentric characters, of whom Cleveland also had its share.

Even with almost daily news stories and heightened awareness, the killings continued. On February 23, 1937, the seventh victim was found. A woman's torso was discovered floating along Kingsbury Run. The body was headless and the arms had been amputated. Victim Seven was also never identified and her death was different from the other murders because she was decapitated after she was killed. The killer also added a grisly touch — he stuffed a pants pocket in her rectum.

A new coroner, Samuel Gerber, had been voted into office. Unlike most coroners of that time, Gerber had a law degree as well as a medical degree. Gerber had never encountered a case like this and it piqued his interest like no other case ever had. Gerber studied all seven decapitation murders. He concurred with Detectives Hogan and Cowles and his predecessor that one person committed all the murders. One question that plagued the coroner and the police officers was: Why did the killer mutilate his victims by cutting off their heads, hands, and arms? Gerber theorized that it was the killer's way of blocking the identification of the victims.

In a report to officers on the case, Gerber gave his assessment of the killer. He wrote that the killer was most likely a doctor. He didn't think the crimes were sexually motivated because the decapitations and dismemberments were too meticulous and the murderer selected both sexes as his victims. He said sexually motivated crimes were usually more frenzied.

Police know today that serial killers develop a *modus operandi* or signature to ensure that their handiwork is recognized, and get credit in their own bizarre way. They also know that these killers love to see their actions reported in the news media. Apparently, it was no different with this killer. Forensic psychiatrists told Eliot Ness that all the coverage may in fact be fueling the killer's zest for killing, or at the very least giving him all the publicity he wanted and would never achieve by any other means.

Ness went to the newspapers and told the editors of his concerns. This must have been hard for Ness because he loved press attention. To his surprise, they agreed to curb back their coverage, particularly the speculation aspects of the case.

This didn't set well with Gerber. In the book, *Eliot Ness — The Real Story*, author Paul Heimel said that almost from the start Gerber and Ness had an antagonistic relationship. Gerber made it known that he didn't agree with the way the case had been handled. And while Ness wanted to keep the case low profile, Gerber turned out to be a bigger media hound than Ness and engaged the press — even offering details of the crimes.

On June 6, 1937, a teenager on his way home from school stumbled upon the skeletal remains of a woman. Coroner Gerber determined that she had been dead for about a year. Victim number eight was the first black victim.

Gerber said in a report that since the body had been treated with quicklime (a substance which dissolved most of the flesh from the bones), he couldn't determine if decapitation was the cause of death. As usual, her arms and legs were never found. Even though the police found a skull with extensive dental work done, her identity was never conclusively determined. Detective Merylo was convinced that the woman was a prostitute named Rose Wallace. She had mysteriously disappeared in the summer of 1936.

## Who Could be the Killer?

Just who was this killer terrorizing the city of Cleveland? Dr. Gerber's analysis was that the killer was a right-handed man with a clear knowledge of anatomy. He used a heavy, sharp knife. Like the detectives on the case, Dr. Gerber thought the killer could be a surgeon, medical student, veterinarian, butcher or even a hunter. He thought the "Mad Butcher" might be bisexual because he killed members of both sexes. Even during modern times, most serial killers have a "specific type" and usually kill members of one sex. Ted Bundy, for example, killed young women with dark hair that they parted in the middle. John Wayne Gacey killed young men.

When Dr. Gerber suggested that it would make sense that the killer was a doctor, the police focused in their investigation on doctors — specifically those they discovered had a penchant for prostitutes, illegal drugs and alcohol, or who were involved with homosexual activity.

The "Mad Butcher" struck again the next month. In July, 1937, the upper portion of a man's torso and two of his thighs were found floating just below Kingsbury Run. The cause of death was decapitation. However, the killer was becoming even more bizarre. This time the killer had also removed all of the victim's abdominal organs and his heart. The organs were removed with surgical precision, which made Gerber think they were definitely dealing with a deranged doctor. However, there was something different about the dismemberment. Gerber noticed that it was not done with the precision of the previous killings. Perhaps the killer was getting sloppy or maybe he was afraid of being discovered.

In his book, *Four Against the Mob*, author Oscar Fraley (who had earlier collaborated with Ness on his book *The Untouchables*) wrote that Ness had told him that he had found a suspect — a doctor that he thought was the killer. However, he couldn't prove it, and he wouldn't tell Fraley who the doctor was.

However, Marilyn Bardsley, in her Internet article titled *Eliot Ness: The Man Behind the Myth*, identifies the suspect. She recounts how Detective Cowles had started a very discrete investigation of the man, Dr. Frank Sweeney.

Dr. Sweeney certainly fit the killer's profile. He was reportedly bisexual and he had a severe drinking problem, which had cost him dearly. His drinking had caused him to lose his surgical residency at a hospital close to Kingsbury Run, and it had also caused his wife to leave him, taking their two children. He was also a large, tall and strong man who had grown up in the Kingsbury Run area. In fact, he had his private practice office in that area at one time. Since Kingsbury Run was the killer's favorite dumping ground, the police had theorized that he was someone who was very familiar with the area.

Sweeney was also the first cousin of Congressman Martin Sweeney. Cowles remained discrete in his investigation, for fear that Congressman Sweeney could make the case that his cousin was being targeted to embarrass him simply because he was a vocal critic of Ness and the Mayor.

Besides, Bardsley reported that Dr. Sweeney always seemed to have an alibi for the estimated time of the murders. He usually had checked himself into a veterans' hospital to treat his drinking problem in a town that was two hours away from Cleveland.

In the meantime, the "Mad Butcher" struck again. During 1937, three more victims were found decapitated. The victims were never identified. Eliot Ness stepped out of the picture of the investigation at this point. Fighting corruption was his forte and he wanted to get back to pursuing it. The other detectives devoted all of their time and effort to solving the crimes. Since trying to find leads on the victims that were not identified proved futile, they reopened the investigations of Edward Andrassy and Florence Polillo; however nothing new was discovered that would aid in the investigation.

Sandusky was a city approximately two hours west of Cleveland. It is the city where the veterans' hospital was located that Dr. Sweeney frequented for his drinking condition. In the spring of 1938, the severed leg of a man was found in this town. When Detective Cowles heard about the latest body, he volunteered to go and investigate.

Bardsley reported that Cowles conducted a discrete investigation and discovered that patients, especially ones of high social standing like Dr. Sweeney, were not strictly monitored or even subjected to confinement. In Sweeney's case, he could probably leave and return at his own choosing.

Cowles desperately wanted to make a connection between the doctor and the murders. Of course, suspecting that Sweeney was the killer and proving it were two entirely different matters.

Through some poking around, Cowles hit pay dirt. The Ohio Penitentiary was near the grounds of the hospital and the prison shared some of the same facilities. Bardsley said that Cowles found an inmate at the penitentiary who claimed he knew Dr. Frank Sweeney very well. Alex Archaki was serving a sentence for burglary and told Cowles that he supplied Dr. Sweeney with liquor during his stays at the hospital, and that Sweeney supplied him with prescription pills. Bardsley reported that Archaki told Cowles that he had met Sweeney in a bar two years prior to his conviction and they had struck up a conversation — albeit a one-sided one from Archaki's perspective. He told Cowles that Sweeney was very curious about his personal life, asking if he was married or had family and friends in the area. Cowles thought that maybe Sweeney was sizing Archaki up to be a victim. He theorized that part of the killer's success so far was in choosing victims who had no immediate family members or friends who would quickly report that they were missing. That certainly was the case with most of his victims so far.

Archaki remembered that there were times when Sweeney disappeared from the hospital — and Cowles determined that those times coincided with the approximate times of death of some of the victims.

As it turned out, the leg found in Sandusky wasn't the result of a murder. Cowles thought that Sweeney would be too smart to kill so close to the place that was his alibi. However, he thought for the first time in this long investigation that he had enough to classify Sweeney as a legitimate suspect.

## Who was Dr. Francis Edward Sweeney?

Before he shared his suspicions about Dr. Sweeney with anyone, including his colleagues, Cowles thought he'd better know more about the doctor. During his investigation he found out that even though Sweeney was the first cousin to Congressman Martin Sweeney, he came from a very poor family. Sweeney had become a doctor against all odds. He had to work hard to put himself through school. He did become a surgical resident and was assigned to a hospital in Kingsbury Run. It was the consensus of those who Cowles had talked with that Sweeney was a good doctor in his residency years and he was an excellent surgeon. He married and had two sons. By all accounts his life was on the upswing and he had a fantastic future ahead of him.

However, something happened to derail that promise. According to his wife, Dr. Sweeney began to drink heavily after only two years of marriage. Eventually, he began to stay drunk all the time, and in September, 1934, they separated. Cowles wondered why a promising doctor would self-destruct. Some people certainly handled pressure and success differently. Cowles found out that Sweeney suffered a head injury during World War I and that alcoholism, as well as mental illness, ran in his family. Cowles noted that the body of the Lady of the Lake was discovered on September 5, 1934 — the same time frame that Sweeney separated from his wife.

Bardsley reported that Cowles was very excited about Sweeney as a suspect. He fit the profile that the investigators had been using as a guide. He was a surgeon, he had lived and worked in the Kingsbury Run area, and knew the place very well. Sweeney was strong and tall, so carrying bodies

---

from one location to another wouldn't be that difficult. Finally, it was rumored that Dr. Sweeney was bisexual — which would explain why the killer selected both sexes as his victims.

Cowles decided to reveal this information to only Eliot Ness and a few members of the investigative team. They agreed they didn't want any word about Dr. Sweeney being a suspect leaking out to the public. They didn't have any concrete evidence and they feared that Congressman Sweeney would indeed say it was a personal attack on him because he had openly criticized Ness' policies.

On April 8, 1938, a woman's leg was found floating in the Cuyahoga River. Ness, Cowles, and the other investigators wanted to investigate further to be sure that this was part of the other murders before reporting it to the press. Ness wanted to keep as much information about the killings from the press as possible. Coroner Gerber didn't agree. He was enjoying being a media darling and immediately told the press that another murder had occurred. This infuriated Ness, and he and Gerber clashed again. He thought that Gerber was using the murders to enhance his own image.

However, Gerber was right. The severed leg did belong to a murdered woman. About a month later, her torso, thighs, and right foot were found in the Cuyahoga River. She was never identified, and her head and arms were never found. Gerber concluded that her death was due to decapitation.

The killings were becoming more frequent. As experts know today, the serial killer becomes bolder as his killings grow in number, and the "cooling off" periods between killings become shorter.

The detectives on the case thought the killer was smart in preventing the police from identifying the victims by destroying their heads and hands (the two most common ways to establish identification). Lack of identification certainly slowed down their investigation. If they knew who the murdered victims were, perhaps they could have uncovered clues as to who they were last seen with. It had been three years and it appeared that the police were getting nowhere. Ness decided to reassign most of the twenty officers.

Bardsley reported that Ness and Cowles decided that it was time to pursue Cowles' suspicions about Dr. Sweeney. A few select investigators were included in the planning session. They thought it was imperative that no word leaked out about their prime suspect. She said the team decided that their next step should be to set up a discrete surveillance of Dr. Sweeney. They decided on a rookie who they thought was trustworthy and wouldn't talk about his assignment.

However, Sweeney was a very savvy man. It took him no time at all to discover that the cop was following him. Sweeney decided to have some fun with his follower one night. He disappeared into a bar patronized almost entirely by blacks. Integration of public places wasn't a common practice then and, of course, the two white men stood out like sore thumbs among the patrons, Sweeney on one side of the bar and the rookie cop keeping his distance on the other side. Naturally, nothing significant came of the surveillance since Sweeney knew he was being followed.

Police thought they had caught a break in the case when another female body was accidentally found at a dump. This time the head and hands were found alongside the rest of the body. Dr. Gerber estimated her death had occurred between February and April. The police were able to lift a fingerprint, but as their luck would have it, there was no matching print on file. The skull and some of the bones of a man were found a couple of hundred feet away from the woman's body. Like the woman, he was dismembered. The detectives weren't sure if these were victims eleven and twelve. If they were, the killer had changed his *modus operandi* in that he had left the hands and heads. He also changed his dumping ground from Kingsbury Run to the Cuyahoga River. These bodies were also not in plain view as the others had been. Cowles was reluctant to categorize these victims as those of the Mad Butcher; even though the bodies were mutilated, the other circumstances were very different. However, since there were enough similarities, Ness thought they were the latest victims. The people of Cleveland believed that the city was indeed in the grips of a madman. They wanted answers or, better yet, they wanted the murderer caught. The press had abandoned their word to scale back their coverage, and the papers were flooded with stories of the murders.

Ness had deliberately tried to keep a hands-off approach when it came to these murders. He was feeling some pressure. Since he was the public safety director, the press and the people started to demand answers from him. Ness realized that he had to do something to achieve some quick results. His next move, which some believe was the biggest mistake of his law enforcement career, was to conduct a raid on the citizens of the Kingsbury Run area. The evening of August 18, 1938, Ness personally led the raid with twenty-six police officers in tow. The police chased and rousted any and all vagrants in the area, took most of them to jail to be fingerprinted and sentenced them to the workhouse. The police then searched the shanties and, when they were done, burned down most of the makeshift homes.

The press was merciless in their criticism of Ness' actions. They sharply criticized Ness for destroying what little these men had and proclaimed that they were being sent to jail for no other reason than that they were poor. They pointed out quite correctly that the raid brought the police no closer to solving the most heinous crimes the city had ever seen. A quote from a newspaper story stated, "The throwing into jail of men broken by experience and the burning of their wretched places of habitation is not likely to lead to the solution of the most macabre mystery in Cleveland history."

Ness' next step, many felt, totally derailed the investigation. Bardsley said he pulled in Dr. Sweeney for questioning. Some, including Detective Cowles, thought that Ness had jumped the gun. At least Cowles was able to convince Ness to conduct the interrogation at a discrete location, possibly to avoid an avalanche of publicity. Sweeney had been on one of his drinking binges and was drying out at one of the city's premier hotels. They all agreed to conduct the questioning there.

Bardsley reported how the chilling encounter went. Ness, along with a court psychiatrist, Detective Cowles, and Dr. Leonard Keller, one of the inventors of the polygraph machine, went to the hotel. Sweeney didn't seem unnerved by the officers. In fact, it looked to Cowles that he reveled in the attention. He was acting as if the investigative team were his guests. Lt. Cowles and Dr. Grossman did most of the questioning. Sweeney was enjoying the exchange, answering questions sometimes jokingly, but mostly very vaguely. When Keller was ready to conduct the polygraph, Cowles gave him a list of questions that included: "Had he ever met Edward Andrassy?" "Did he kill him?" "Did he kill Florence Polillo?"

Keller took Sweeney into the bedroom to conduct the questioning. When he was done, he called Ness aside. He told Ness that he was confident that Dr. Frank Sweeney was the killer. Ness conferred with Dr. Grossman because he could hardly believe that this intelligent man, a doctor, was

---

the Mad Butcher. Dr. Grossman told Ness he thought that Sweeney was severely mentally disturbed and a psychopath.

Ness told the others that he wanted to talk to Sweeney alone. The men went to a coffee shop next door. When Ness entered the bedroom, Sweeney gave him a big grin. Ness told him he thought that he was the killer. Sweeney came scarily close to Ness and said, "Then prove it." Bardsley said in her report that Ness had faced down killers like Al Capone, but there was something scarier about Sweeney, and he immediately got on the phone and called for the others to return.

To be sure, Ness wanted Keeler to retest Sweeney several times. The results did not change. Even though Ness and the others in the room thought they had the killer, they couldn't prove it —Sweeney was right.

Ness knew at best that all they had was circumstantial evidence. There was no weapon, no witnesses that could place Sweeney with any of the victims, and no bloody clothes. It was well before the time of fiber examinations and DNA tests.

The murders stopped in August, 1938, as mysteriously as they started. Was it because two days after the hotel inquiry (August 2, 1938) Dr. Sweeney committed himself to the veterans' hospital in Sandusky? He remained committed in several hospitals until his death in 1965. Since he had committed himself, he was free to leave the hospital grounds for weeks or sometimes months, but he always returned. Other similar murders were committed in other states, but no connection to Sweeney was ever found. Bardsley said when he left the hospitals (specifically Sandusky Veterans' Hospital), hospital personnel were instructed to contact the police in the Cleveland and Sandusky areas.

In 1955, Sweeney transferred to a hospital in Dayton, Ohio, where he remained until he died. Sweeney's behavior became even stranger over the years. Consumed by his alcoholism, he would send taunting post cards to Eliot Ness.

However, the questions still remain. Why did Sweeney voluntarily commit himself to hospitals? Was he even a viable suspect? Did Ness make a deal with Sweeney's cousin, the congressman, to put the doctor away to end the killings? For Ness, a deal would have meant putting a stop to the killings and getting on with his important task of fighting corruption and racketeering. And with the killings stopped, the press would focus on his more successful efforts. For Congressman Sweeney, a deal would have meant sparing him from the embarrassment of having a murderer in the family, and, most importantly, save his political career.

Oscar Fraley said in his book that Ness told him he couldn't prove that the suspect committed the crimes and, because the man had strong political connections, he allowed him to be committed to a mental hospital.

Bradley reported that most people who knew Dr. Sweeney insisted that he was not the killer — just a tragic, lonely man who let a potentially great life disappear through his fingers. For Ness, however, it was the one case that he couldn't bring to justice. His law enforcement career was never the same after the case. According to the A&E *Biography* special, his reputation survived not solving one of the biggest murder cases of that decade, but eventually his reputation began to falter. While the press initially loved him when he first came to Cleveland and reported on his corruption fighting efforts, they started reporting on his nightlife of dancing and drinking. Ness apparently had developed a very serious drinking problem.

Two months after a hit-and-run car accident where Ness was at fault, he resigned from his job. He eventually ran for mayor but lost by a huge margin. His mayoral campaign left him broke and dejected. He met Oscar Fraley, and after Ness regaled him with stories about Chicago and his fight against liquor, they collaborated on the book *The Untouchables.*

The book wasn't an initial success and many criticized it, accusing Ness and Fraley of extremely embellishing Ness' exploits. However, a television series based on the book and starring Robert Stack was a huge success, but Ness would never realize what status he had achieved because he died of a heart attack in 1957 at age fifty-three, before the show premiered.

## Were There Other Viable Suspects?

The case officially ended in 1938. One of the detectives, Peter Merylo, continued to pursue the case without any success. There were no more credible suspects, even though a later investigation by a subsequent sheriff centered on an alcoholic named Frank Dolezal. Even though the man had confessed to killing Flo Polillo, it became obvious that the confession was coerced. He even kept changing his confession to match the facts of the case. After being held in jail for almost a week, his family hired him a lawyer and the man recanted his confession, saying he was beaten by the law enforcement officers until he confessed. There was no evidence to support the confession. On a sad note, Dolezal was found hanging in his cell. An autopsy revealed that he had been severely beaten at the time of his arrest and that he was left hanging for more than fifteen minutes.

## Interview with Captain Michael Nault

Captain Nault is a major crimes investigator who is an expert in the field of tracking down serial killers. He's commanded the investigation of such serial killings as the Green River serial killings that are profiled in Chapter Nine of this book. It was in handling that case that Nault developed a personal interest in psychopaths. He's a lecturer for police departments across the country and federal law enforcement agencies such as the FBI and internationally. He has taught classes on the subject to police departments, the FBI academy, and Scotland Yard, to name a few. He also lectures nationally and internationally on policing and on how to identify serial killers.

Here's what he had to say about the Cleveland Kingsbury Run murders: "First, let me say I think the officers in this case did a lot of things right," even though they were hampered by not knowing some of the nuances of investigating a serial killing.

"They proceeded cautiously and quietly — recognizing they were not dealing with a typical homicide," said Nault.

Of course, on the flip side, Nault said probably the biggest mistake the investigators made was searching for a motive and looking for a suspect in the victims' backgrounds.

"Even today, some police departments make that mistake when they are confronted with the possibility of a serial killing," said Nault. "We're discovering more and more about the makeup of serial killers. There are factors that distinguish a crime as a serial killing — which include that the killer is usually relationless to the victim, the incidents are separated by time (a cooling-off period), and the motive is believed to be the murderer's desire to have power over the victims."

Nault has been involved with many serial killing cases, including the capture of George Russell, who believed he would be the first African-American serial killer. During 1989-1990 Russell was accused of killing three women in Bellevue, Washington. Russell was eventually arrested, tried, and convicted of the murders. Nault said it was the quick action of the Bellevue police and their willingness to accept the premise that they had a serial murderer on their hands that allowed Russell to be captured after a relatively short spree.

Nault said that despite some minor differences between the killings or using different dumping sites for some of the victims in the Kingsbury Run murders, he thinks it was only one killer, and he adds that it's a distinct possibility that the killer was Dr. Sweeney.

"Based on what I read here, I think the killer could very well have been Dr. Sweeney. He certainly demonstrated all of the smug characteristics that serial killers have; for example, his toying with the police. He also had a habit of creating alibis — from what I read here he seemed truly psychopathic. I think by today's standards the case was very solvable. Perhaps with DNA matching or fingerprint comparison — somehow he could have been connected to the murders," said Nault. "As far as the differences in some of the murders' it's not unusual for serial killers to change their MO when the pressure is on."

If profiling had been more widely accepted, would this have made a difference in the case? Nault said no — he's not a big advocate of profiling. "The trouble with profiling is that the profile is usually so broad that it's not very useful. And, the profile is only correct about 17 percent of the time."

The killer in the Cleveland murders killed both men and women and according to Nault that is not necessarily unusual. "His anger was not gender-focused, therefore victims

were picked randomly. Just as with the Green River killer —
his spree was not racially focused, but was gender-focused
on prostitutes. They will often kill a sample just to let the police know that their 'issue' is not gender, race, or anything
else," he said.

Dr. Sweeney died in 1965, but before his death there were
similar murders in other parts of the country. Is it possible
that a serial killer can suddenly stop the killing or do they
simply move on?

"There is a popular tendency to think one killer is good for
all — that's not so. Serial killers *usually* don't travel to different states (there are exceptions, of course, most notably
Ted Bundy)," said Nault. "They can stop for a while under
pressure — but they *have to* resume killing eventually because it is their only form of self-actualization."

# Chapter Four
# The Death of Superman

Superman could bend steel with his bare hands and leap tall buildings in a single bound — or so the introduction to the hit television series said. Unfortunately, for George Reeves, the actor who portrayed Superman, he wasn't faster than a speeding bullet.

When the Los Angeles police responded to a frantic call in the early morning of June 16, 1959, they found Reeves' nude body laying on its back. A bullet from a .38-caliber pistol had ripped through his skull and exited, ending up in the ceiling of the room.

Reeves' fiancé Lenore Lemmon told police that they were having a small party to celebrate their impending marriage (they were to be married June 19 in Mexico). She told the detectives that around 1:15 a.m., Reeves had complained of a severe headache and went upstairs to bed. The rest of the guests remained downstairs.

Lemmon said Reeves had been drinking heavily; in fact, toxicology reports conducted on him indicated that his blood-alcohol level registered a .27, almost three times the legal definition for intoxication. The tests also revealed that Reeves was also taking painkillers for an injury he suffered in a car accident a month earlier. Reeves' head was thrown through the car windshield. He needed several stitches and was still suffering from blindingly painful headaches. Lemmon said soon after Reeves went upstairs, they heard a gunshot, ran upstairs, and found Reeves. The coroner officially ruled Reeves' death as a suicide.

*George Reeves as Superman*

## The Case Against Suicide

However, when police searched the room, they discovered two additional bullet holes in the walls of the bedroom. There were no powder residues found around Reeves' wound, there was no suicide note, there were no powder burns on Reeves' hand, reportedly there were no fingerprints on the gun, and the gun was found at his feet. According to Jim Nolt, the perennial Reeves historian and expert, reports have indicated that Reeves was shot from more than sixteen inches away and his body was lying face up.

## Reeves' Beginnings

Reeves was born in 1914 in Woodstock, Illinois, as George Bessolo. While in high school he discovered his penchant for acting. While in college he was appearing in a play when a studio executive saw him, recognized his potential and signed him to a deal with Warner Brothers Studios. "Bessolo" sounded ethnic, and at the suggestion of studio executives he changed his name to Reeves.

By the time the Superman role came about, Reeves had compiled an impressive list of film credits. He had roles in such films as *Gone With The Wind*, *The Fighting 69$^{th}$* starring James Cagney, and *So Proudly We Hail* with Claudette Colbert (which was one of his biggest roles).

His film career was burgeoning when World War II started. Reeves was called to serve and because of his background was asked to appear in a number of training films, which he gladly did.

However, when he returned from the service, Reeves had been forgotten and his brand of charm was no longer what audiences wanted. While he struggled to restart his film career, in 1951, Reeves received a big break and won the title role in the television series *The Adventures of Superman.* The series was an immediate hit, and the success of the show may have taken Reeves by surprise. However, sometimes a successful series can be a double-edged sword. According to an A&E *Biography,* Reeves loved to act and he loved the steady paycheck of a weekly series. However, he felt the role was very limiting for an actor and it offered few challenges. After all, his character was based on a comic book superhero.

In the same special, Jack Larson, the actor who portrayed cub reporter Jimmy Olson, said that Reeves thought the role was silly and he hated the costume. According to Larson, to add to the illusion of physical superiority, extra muscle padding was added, which made the costume hot and bulky. In later years, Reeves had trouble controlling his weight for the revealing tights. Larson said that the stunts required for the role were dangerous. He said Reeves almost injured himself several times, especially during the stunts that were used for flying scenes. Once a wire snapped and Reeves fell through some glass. He wasn't seriously hurt, but such stunts could have led to some very serious injuries. Larson explained that Reeves finally put his foot down, and in later episodes there were very few dangerous stunts and less flying scenes.

Still, Reeves seemed to enjoy the perks of being a television star. He had met his wife in college and they were married in 1940. They divorced nine years later, making Reeves a handsome, eligible bachelor during the heyday of the television series. Even though the television show was aimed squarely at children, Reeves' nights were filled with late-night partying. Reeves evidently loved the company and the attention of the ladies. All-night drinking parties at his home were not uncommon. He also loved the nightlife of the party capital of the world: Los Angeles.

## If Murder — Who are the Suspects?

It was during one of these partygoing occasions that Reeves met and embarked on a long-term affair with Toni Mannix — a woman ten years his senior. She was married to a powerful MGM executive named Eddie Mannix. Eddie Mannix reportedly had powerful mob connections. Toni apparently really loved Reeves and being a wealthy woman she subsidized Reeves' lavish lifestyle. According to Jim Nolt their affair was very well-known in Hollywood. She had a key to his house and he was a welcome guest at the couple's home.

Their affair continued for ten years, but then Reeves met an attractive 35-year-old New Yorker named Lenore Lemmon. Their relationship was a passionate one and can best be termed volatile — they argued frequently, according to Nolt.

Lemmon was a jealous woman and Reeves was a recognizable, handsome television star. According to the A&E *Biography*, Lemmon became enraged when other women recognized or wanted to talk with Reeves. Being an old-fashioned star, Reeves often went out of his way to talk with his fans, which further enraged Lemmon.

The circumstances of Reeve's death remain a mystery mostly because of his personal life. Reeves apparently had many simultaneous affairs, which are described in detail in the book *Hollywood Kryptonite*. Did he have an affair with a jealous or married woman, and was she or her husband looking for revenge?

Lemmon apparently was extremely jealous of the still-warm feelings that Reeves held for Toni Mannix. She said in interviews after Reeves' death that Toni Mannix didn't let go of Reeves the couple after their breakup.

In 1957, the *Superman* series wrapped production. Larson said in the *Biography* special that Reeves was happy that the show was ending. He had grown tired of playing the superhero and was excited at the prospect of being able to act in meatier, more meaningful roles. However, in an ironic twist of fate, the role that had made him a star had severely typecast him. The roles that he coveted were not forthcoming. Producers were extremely reluctant to cast Reeves because they were concerned that audiences would identify him with his Superman persona. And, in the 1950s, it was hard for actors to make the transition from the television screen to the movie screen. Television actors were definitely considered lesser in stature than film actors.

By 1959, Reeves was feeling the effects of not having steady paychecks. He had enjoyed an expensive lifestyle, and he didn't have Toni Mannix by his side to help with that expense. However, his friends say that suicide was the last thing on Reeves' mind because his prospects were looking up. He had accepted a role in an upcoming film that was shooting in Spain and the creators of *The Adventures of Superman* had decided to produce another season of the show — Reeves agreed and his career seemed on track again.

One of the people most fervent in the belief that Reeves was murdered was his mother, Helen Bessolo. She said she believed that her son was murdered because he had no reason to commit suicide. Even though she hadn't spoken with her son for almost a week before his death, she insisted that he was looking forward to all aspects of his life — both professionally and personally.

Mrs. Bessolo refused to have her son cremated for three years while she tried to find answers to his tragic death. She hired a private detective to investigate. However, the only information that the investigator reported to her was the discovery of the additional bullet holes.

## What the Expert Says

Jim Nolt is one of the foremost historians on George Reeves. He has conducted hours of research on Reeves and his tragic death. I talked with him from his home in Pennsylvania about his thoughts on what really happened to George

Reeves, and why his death still fascinates all these years later.

"I always felt that there was something special about George Reeves. I, like most people, liked the quiet strength he portrayed and the sense of dignity and genuine warmth that he brought out in the character of Superman. I think people were drawn to him and liked him for those reasons," he said. Nolt believes that despite numerous accounts that Reeves detested portraying the character of Superman, all of his research indicates that Reeves liked the role and took it very seriously.

Nolt says there are three theories in Reeves' death, but there is only one he truly believes. The first theory — "George may have committed suicide because he had not worked for some time. He had been involved in a traffic accident, and was in a great deal of pain," he said. Toxicology reports indicated that he was taking pain medication at the time of his death. Nolt continued by explaining that Lenore was a party girl, and there was constant drinking the last months of Reeves' life. "Sometimes alcohol, especially mixed with pain medication, has a way of distorting your view of life and modifying your behavior," said Nolt. However, Nolt said he doubts that Reeves would resort to suicide. "He enjoyed living too much and his acting career was definitely turning around."

The second theory, Nolt says, is that Toni Mannix or Eddie Mannix killed Reeves. Toni Mannix was reportedly devastated by the breakup with Reeves and may have used her husband's connections to kill Reeves. "They had a long-term affair and she really cared about George. Was Toni angry enough to kill him? Yes, but did she? I doubt it," said Nolt. "And as for Eddie, the affair between Toni and George was well known to everyone in Hollywood, including Eddie, who apparently didn't object because George was a welcome guest at the Mannixes' home." Nolt said the three even went on vacations together. "Eddie always had other companions, also. Toni and Eddie had a unique marriage. They were not a happily married couple that George came between. I don't know why they were married — perhaps it was some kind of financial arrangement, but they both seemed to enjoy outside relationships. So Eddie was not in some jealous rage over George."

The third scenario is that the killer was Lenore Lemmon. "I personally think that Lenore Lemmon killed George. I don't think he was going to marry her," said Nolt. However, most published accounts said that Reeves was looking forward to his wedding. Nolt responded by explaining that Lemmon had alienated him from most of his close friends in the last six months of his life. "Lenore had isolated George from most of his friends, so I think we don't know what he was feeling leading up to his death. But, some of his friends said that George was tiring of her antics, and maybe realized that he really didn't love her. I think it was very unlikely that he was going to marry her," said Nolt. "She was a person who was very used to having and getting her own way." Nolt said she was extremely jealous, and would go into a rage when other women paid attention to Reeves. He said Reeves was a very outgoing man and liked reaching out to his fans, and Lemmon's behavior was a source of embarrassment to Reeves.

He said that the relationship between Reeves and Lemmon was very volatile. "As a matter of fact, the night that George died they were seen at a restaurant arguing and mere hours later George was dead. I think the argument continued when they got home and she eventually lost it during the evening and shot him."

Nolt admits that there are holes in all three scenarios. For example, there were three other people at the house that night when the police arrived — why would they go along with a suicide story?

"They were all very drunk that night. They didn't call the police for more than forty minutes after they supposedly discovered the body. I think they needed that time to sober up. With everyone being drunk, it would have been easy for Lenore to slip out of the room, shoot George, and then return to the party. The others may have supported the suicide story because that's what Lenore had told them and they were too drunk to know any differently," Nolt said.

He points out that even though three bullet holes were found in the bedroom only one shell casing was found, and it was under Reeves' body. Lemmon had an explanation for the police. She claimed that she had been playing around when the gun accidentally went off. "Personally, I think somebody tried to clean up and removed the other two casings, but didn't remove the third one in order to fit in with the suicide story."

Nolt said the police didn't check to see if there were other rounds in the gun chamber, and there were no powder burns on Reeves' hand or around the wound.

Nolt also said that the police did very little to investigate Reeves' death. "Lenore Lemmon told them the suicide story and they merely accepted it," he said. "The only test that was done was the blood-alcohol one. George's body was embalmed before his mother even reached California. We only have Lenore Lemmon's word as to what happened that night. It certainly isn't backed up by any scientific evidence."

Nolt said that through the years there have been speculation that there may have been others in the house that night but the police did nothing to follow up on those allegations.

"I think the police didn't investigate George's death more thoroughly because they weren't allowed to," said Nolt.

Of course in those days, studios went out of their way to protect their stars. A huge scandal such as the murder of one of the most beloved television stars could have been very bad for business, so they could have called off the investigation.

Nolt points out that both Lemmon and Toni Mannix had powerful police connections. "Part of Eddie Mannix's job at the studio was to "handle" the police when the stars got into trouble. Part of his job was to protect the stars and the studio, so he was very skilled at knowing how to kill an investigation. However, if Eddie or Toni did kill George, they took that information to their graves."

"Lenore Lemmon also had powerful police connections, but mostly on the East Coast," said Nolt. But it would seem logical that she called someone on the East Coast, who then called someone in the police department out in California.

Initially, Jack Larson, along with other members of the Superman cast, staunchly argued against the idea that George Reeves committed suicide. Larson and Noel Neill, who portrayed Lois Lane, made the talk show rounds disputing the suicide finding.

However, now Larson has changed his mind and says he believes that George Reeves took his own life. "I was the technical expert for the television program *Unsolved Mysteries* when they did a segment on George," said Nolt. Jack and I were sitting alone and he told me he thought George had been murdered. But when he appeared on camera he said George had been very despondent and probably committed suicide."

Why the dramatic turnaround? "I think Jack Larson simply got tired of trying to explain who might have killed George," said Nolt.

In a final twist, Reeves left almost his entire estate to Toni Mannix. Neither his mother nor Lenore Lemmon were remembered in his will. "Lenore had said that there was another will, but no other wills were ever found. I believe George never intended to leave her anything, and he wanted Toni to have everything," said Nolt.

Lenore Lemmon left California and moved back to New York, where she lived until she was found dead in her apartment on New Year's Day, 1991. Helen Bessolo had died in 1964, never unraveling the mystery of what happened to her son.

# Chapter Five
# Hogan's Heroes' Star
# Lives and Dies Bizarrely

*Bob Crane as Colonel Robert Hogan*

Hollywood has a way of using people up and then tossing them out. Actor Bob Crane, former sitcom star of the hit television series *Hogan's Heroes* was on top of the entertainment world in the 1960s. However, by the time of his death on June 29, 1978, Hollywood had turned its back on the 49-year-old actor. He was traveling around the country, performing in dinner theatres making about $300 a week, and living a sleazy sexual lifestyle, even by Hollywood standards.

Crane was performing in a play titled *Beginner's Luck* at The Windmill Theater, and was found brutally murdered in his hotel room in Scottsdale, Arizona. His face was beaten to the point where one side was practically caved in. Investigators concluded that Crane was viciously beaten with a blunt object. They also made another discovery that would prove to shock the fans of the wholesome-appearing Crane. There were well over fifty homemade porno movies in the room starring Crane performing in the sex acts, and many photographs of nude women posing for the camera or having sex with Crane.

Crane had developed an interest in electronics dating back to his radio days. He often made home movies of his family in those early days, but these were no family movies. He had apparently used his time out of the spotlight to integrate his passions — electronics, a lust for many women, performing, and pornography.

Many television actors who had had successful television series became so closely connected with the character they portrayed that they were horribly typecast. It happened to George Reeves as Superman, whose untimely death is recounted in Chapter Four of this book. It happened to countless others and it happened to Bob Crane.

When the news of Crane's death was reported, it was revealed that the image of the all-American, wholesome persona was a façade. The A&E *Biography* of Crane's life, titled *Bob Crane: A Double Life,* revealed an accurate description of what Crane's life had become. Traveling the road back from stardom, Crane's personal life had taken a bizarre turn that consisted of having sex with many women while videotaping the act. It was evident from the tapes that some of the women were more than willing, but some probably didn't suspect that their performance was being recorded on camera.

## Crane's Rise to Fame

Bob Crane was born on July 13, 1928, in Waterbury, Connecticut. He loved music and in his youth dreamed of a career as a professional drummer. By the time he was 16 years old Crane had dropped out of high school and had gotten a job as the drummer for a symphony orchestra. After two years Crane left the orchestra to pursue other opportunities. He supported himself by working along the East Coast as a drummer.

Crane married his high school sweetheart, Anne, during this time. Realizing the responsibilities of marriage, Crane got a steadier job as a radio announcer at a small station in Hornell, New York. It was there that Crane's show business career blossomed. Crane showed a flair for comedy and his show became the top-rated program. He developed a comedy routine that earned him the attention of radio stations in larger cities and after working in radio for six years, Crane decided he was ready to pursue an acting career. He and his wife packed up their belongings and headed for Los Angeles.

He started working for station KNX in Los Angeles doing the morning drive timeslot. Crane's off-the-cuff humor and quick wit made him an immediate favorite among radio listeners, and he was soon making a six-figure salary, which back in 1956 was no small feat for a radio personality.

Crane was ambitious and a hard worker. His wife complained that he devoted so much time and effort working on material for his career that he had little time for anything else. She also said Crane had little time for drinking, smoking or partying — a far cry from the man he had become by the time he was killed.

During the 1960s, Crane had made the leap from radio to television doing guest appearances on such programs as *The Jack Benny Show, The Ed Sullivan Show* and *The Dick Van Dyke Show*. Crane was a big hit and was always a welcome guest.

Donna Reed had seen some of Crane's television performances and was impressed by his comedic talents. She asked him to appear on her hit show. He accepted and became a regular, portraying neighbor Dr. Dave Kelsey from 1963-1965. His wife had said that he liked the wholesome nature of the program. Apparently in those days Crane had said that he detested salaciousness and only went to movies or watched television programs that his kids could enjoy. Crane also took turns as a dramatic actor, guest starring on episodes of *Night Gallery* and *The Twilight Zone*.

But along the way Crane's values started to change. While still on the Reed show, he reportedly grew tired of the show's squeaky-clean image and wanted to perform in racier programs. Crane left *The Donna Reed Show* and auditioned for and got the part that would make him a major television star — that of Colonel Robert Hogan. *Hogan's Heroes* debuted in 1965 and ran for six seasons. It was set in a German prisoner of war camp during World War II. The premise of the show was that a group of POWs, led by the wisecracking Colonel Hogan, actually ran an underground sabotage operation right under the nose of the not-so-bright German Commander, Colonel Klink, and the even dimmer Sergeant Schultz. The POWs were constantly outwitting the Germans, and audiences loved it. The show was an instant hit and made a star of Crane. The series had provided Crane with what most people in that industry wanted — fame, fortune, and respect. That respect earned Crane two Emmy nominations in 1966 and 1967.

*The cast of Hogan's Heroes*

It was an ensemble cast, but the show was centered squarely on Crane. His natural affability and charisma helped the show to remain a top ratings winner for the network for almost its entire run. Crane had also engaged in numerous affairs during the television series. With his success and affairs, things started to change in his personal life. In 1970, Crane ended his marriage of twenty-one years. He and Anne had two children, but his numerous affairs had taken its toll on the marriage.

One of Crane's affairs had been with his co-star on *Hogan's Heroes*, Patti Olsen (she portrayed Colonel Klink's secretary, Hilda) and they got married four months after his divorce from Anne.

When *Hogan's Heroes* was cancelled, many producers in the industry worried that Bob Crane was too connected with the character of Colonel Hogan, and he had trouble finding work during the post-*Hogan's Heroes* years.

Crane, however, had good representation, and unlike some stars of that time period, he received a part of the syndication rights, so money wasn't a problem. But finding work in the industry was. He tried movie projects such as *Superdad* and *Gus*, and both fizzled at the box office. He tried television again with *The Bob Crane Show* — but the show was cancelled after only thirteen episodes.

However, Crane seemed to have found another outlet for his creativity. His sexual appetites became kinky and maybe even disturbed. Crane wasn't content with having affairs — he often had gratuitous sexual encounters, usually one night stands, with more than one woman at once — and all for the benefit of his ever-present video camera.

The one question is, why? Many feel that the effects of middle age, a dead career, and not being able to cope with the fact that he wasn't a top television star anymore, fueled

Crane's deep obsession for kinky sex and pornography. Maybe it massaged his deflated ego or filled an empty void.

In the MSNBC program titled *Crime Files,* Ed Beck, a minister and friend of Crane, said that Crane had a sex addiction. For whatever the reason, it was the 70s — pre-AIDS awareness and the height of sexual freedom, and Crane took full advantage of the times. He even took out ads in swingers magazines advertising for willing partners, and from the tapes that police found in his home, he got plenty of responses.

Beck said that Crane's behavior had gotten so out of control that he started reliving his conquests by showing his homemade porno movies to strangers, or anyone for that matter, who would share the experience with him.

## Partner in Crime

Crane had met and befriended an unattractive, uncharismatic videotape equipment salesman on the set of *Hogan's Heroes.* John Henry Carpenter was an eager and willing participant in Crane's passion for making homemade porno movies. Some reports indicate that at times Carpenter would hide in a closet or another room and tape Crane and the women having sex. Carpenter, more often though, took part in the sex with the women, often participating in threesomes or foursomes or any number of combinations. The two became good friends or at least they developed a friendship largely built on their mutual passion for electronic equipment and videotape sex.

The one big difference, however, was that without Crane's charm and celebrity (although fading), the unattractive, and some say creepy, Carpenter wouldn't have stood a chance in getting women to participate. Crane would often share his conquests with Carpenter, and the women would go along to please Crane or to be the next one to have sex with him.

On the *Biography* special, Crane's daughter said Carpenter loved the fringe benefits of being her father's friend. And Carpenter reveled in his friendship with Crane. While Crane was playing dinner theaters around the country, Carpenter would often fly from Los Angeles to whatever city Crane was performing in, and the two would cruise the town looking to pick up women. Through Crane, Carpenter had achieved what he otherwise couldn't — he was instantly accepted in circles to which he would not have otherwise had access, and he had women willing to participate in kinky sexual behavior. "He was definitely a hanger-on," said Crane's son Robert in the *Biography* special.

By 1978, Crane had separated from his second wife and he was free to engage in casual sexual encounters, going to strip clubs and topless bars without remorse or guilt. Which he did anyway while he was still living with his wife.

## What Happened That Night?

From all accounts June 29 was a typical day for Bob Crane. He attended rehearsal and then performed in *Beginner's Luck*. Afterwards he and Carpenter got together for a night of wild sex. It has been reported that the two would share one woman with each man taking his turn with her, or they would get more than one woman and have sex with them in the same room.

They went to a bar and met up with two women. For whatever reason Crane didn't follow his routine of taking the woman back to his room for videotaped sex. After dinner he

---

apparently took his date home and returned to his hotel room, alone. When Crane didn't show up for rehearsal the next day, a fellow cast member went to find out what was wrong. Investigators said after knocking and getting no answer the door was unlocked so she walked in. She approached Crane's bedroom and made the grisly discovery — Crane's bloody body in bed. She ran out calling for help.

When the police arrived the place was a bloody mess. They didn't find a murder weapon, but what they did find was Bob Crane. In addition to being viciously beaten about the face and head, in an ironic twist, a cord from a video camera was tied around his neck. The detectives believed that someone slipped into Crane's room in the middle of the night. Crane was in bed when he was viciously beaten.

Police immediately suspected John Carpenter, but when questioned he said that he and Crane had parted ways earlier that evening. He said after they left the restaurant he went back to his hotel room and packed because he was leaving the next day. He said he called Crane around 3:00 a.m. to tell him that he was driving himself to the airport the next morning.

The police didn't believe his story. Carpenter was staying only one block away from Crane's apartment. They believed that Carpenter went over to talk to Crane in person and they argued.

When Carpenter returned his rent-a-car, he left specific instructions that the car be thoroughly cleaned. When detectives examined the car they found a blood streak along the door. When the blood was tested, it was type "B" — Bob Crane's blood type.

However, with no murder weapon, no witnesses, and a lack of a credible motive, it would take years before police were able to build a case against Carpenter.

## If Carpenter was the Killer,
## What was the Motive?

Investigators surmised that Carpenter had grown increasingly resentful of Crane's easy way with women and Crane's growing refusal (or maybe the women's refusal) to share the women with Carpenter. Ed Beck, who also managed the Windmill Theatre, said on the *Crime Files* special that Crane wanted to change his life and was trying to distance himself from Carpenter. He said that Crane was coming to him for guidance and told him that the lifestyle he was leading held no passion for him anymore. Beck said he told Crane if he really wanted to change, he needed to sever his destructive ties, and that meant friendships that were keeping him connected with that lifestyle.

In that same special, Crane's son Robert said his father told him that he had grown tired of his friendship with Carpenter, and that he was going to tell him that their friendship was over. Police believe that would have been devastating news for Carpenter. A lot of his identity was wrapped up in being Bob Crane's friend.

The police had reports that Carpenter and Crane were seen having a heated argument at a bar the day before Crane was murdered. They think the argument continued the next night, and Carpenter became violently deranged and beat Crane to death.

Although Carpenter was the main suspect in the case, it took authorities fourteen years to bring an indictment against him for Crane's murder. Photographs were taken of Carpenter's rented car during the initial investigation. In 1990, a new prosecutor was reviewing the photographs and found what he thought was evidence that was overlooked during the initial investigation. The photo revealed what appeared to be a piece of human tissue (probably from Crane's brain) on the car seat. Armed with this new evidence, prosecutors sought and got an indictment against Carpenter two years later for Crane's murder.

During the trial, a forensic expert testified that he believed it was human tissue in the photograph. However, it was revealed that the tissue was never preserved or personally examined. With the advent of DNA testing, the blood they found on Carpenter's car was retested, but the results were inconclusive as to whether it was Bob Crane's. One juror said that they needed more tangible evidence before they were willing to convict a man of murder charges, and Carpenter was acquitted. Carpenter died in 1998 at age seventy. He denied having anything to do with Bob Crane's death all the way to the end of his life.

Bob Crane's murder remains unsolved — there were other theories on who might have killed him. One was that it was a jealous husband of one of the women he had sex with. Another theory was that it was one of the women he had videotaped who wanted the tape and killed Crane when he wouldn't turn it over. However, investigators had said that it was unlikely that the killer could have been a woman, because the force of the blows to Crane's head would have taken a great deal of strength.

As for the murder weapon, police later discovered that a camera tripod was missing from Crane's room when they arrived to investigate the next day. Friends remembered Crane having two and only one was found in his room.

It was a vicious beating that Crane endured. Ed Beck was called in to make the identification and said that one side of Crane's face was beaten so severely that he was unrecognizable. Beck said he couldn't make the identification until authorities turned his body over to the other side.

Investigators on the case, and most of Crane's family and friends, believe it was Carpenter who murdered Bob Crane. Robert Crane said after Carpenter's acquittal that nothing in his father's life, either personally or publicly, warranted him being murdered, a sentiment with which his friends and co-stars agreed.

Perhaps we'll never know what actually happened the night Crane was murdered, but his persona as the affable Colonel Hogan lives on.

---

# Chapter Six
# Unique Perspectives on Crime

*Gregg Olsen*

## A View of Crime from Gregg Olsen

Why are we, the public, so interested in crime and what makes a good crime story? I decided to ask prolific true crime writer Gregg Olsen his thoughts on these questions.

Olsen is the author of numerous non-fiction books. His investigative true crime books have earned him critical acclaim for their research, characterization and telling the story in a spellbinding way.

His books include *If Loving You Is Wrong; The Confessions of an American Black Widow (A True Story of Greed, Lust and a Murderous Wife); Starvation Heights: The True Story of an American Doctor and the Murder of an English Heiress; Mockingbird: a Mother, a Child, A Tragedy; Bitter Almonds: The True Story of Mothers, Daughters, and the Seattle Cyanide Murders;* and the best-selling *Abandoned Prayers: The True Story of Murder, Obsession and Little Boy Blue.*

What are the components of an intriguing crime story? "I think when people read about true crime stories, they want the whole package — that being the truth, the tragedy and hopefully redemption. But murder is oftentimes more complicated," said Olsen. "When I choose to write on a subject, it has to be something personal for me. For example, most of the books I've written are about women, such as Mary Kay Letourneau and Sharon Lynn Nelson. I like to delve into their characters — their makeup — and explore what drives a person who seemingly has a normal life to commit murder."

He explained that it intrigues people because we usually think of women as nurturers or particularly caring. "When we realize that a woman committed a diabolical act such as murder, it really pushes the intrigue button."

Another interesting factor for female killers, according to Olsen, is the way they commit a crime. "Their method is non-violent in a sense because more often than not they engage in some kind of passive act. For example, in my book, *Starvation Heights*, the woman starved her victims to death, or in the book, *Bitter Almonds,* she poisoned her victims." Olsen said that, make no mistake about it, the victims are just as dead, but it's the method that is so intriguing.

Another interesting factor, according to Olsen, is the downfall of people who seem to have it all. He cites the example of someone like Ted Bundy, the serial killer who appeared to have a great life ahead of him in the form of career, charisma, and friends — but it all went terribly wrong.

"Or take the case of Mary Kay LaTourneau, the subject of the book, *If Loving You Is Wrong*. She was a teacher who was convicted of having sex (and eventually two children) with one of her students when he was only thirteen years old," said Olsen. "On the surface she was a woman with a normal life, a husband, four kids, and a job she loved. She committed this crime out of some kind of emotional need."

Another case involved Tanya Reid. She was at the center of Olsen's book, *Mockingbird: A Mother, A Child, A Tragedy*. She succeeded in killing one of her children and had attempted to kill the others. Olsen said she suffered from a condition known as "Munchausen's by Proxy Syndrome." It usually involves a parent causing harm to their children and rushing them to a hospital or doctor's office, presumably just in time to save the child's life. They act as a devoted parent who is constantly caring for, and trying to find the cause of their child's illness.

"In Reid's case, she suffocated her children to try for that attention. She was usually able to revive the children and got a lot of notice and recognition for her supposed bravery. During my investigation I discovered something very interesting. When she was in high school she was babysitting and the kid stopped breathing. She performed CPR and saved the child's life. Tanya Reid was put in the spotlight. She was recognized at a school assembly and won an award. Who knows — that attention could have triggered some kind of emotional need in her," said Olsen.

Another component that contributes to a good crime story, according to Olsen, is the lifestyle of the people involved. "If they are wealthy, attractive and educated — people who seem to have it all — it's fascinating because we want to know what went wrong," he said, adding that the book he is currently working on fits that category. When he was researching an idea for a book he came across an old newspaper clipping about a 10-year old boy, a prominent doctor's son, who was forcibly taken from his home two days after Christmas in 1936.

"I've tentatively titled the book *The Kidnapped Boy*. It was an incredible story that touched me in the most profound way. As I sat looking at a photograph of the smiling Charlie Mattson, somehow it reached out to me. He was sitting on a pony, and there appeared to be no end to his smile. I knew I had to tell the story, because it's been largely untold and it's unsolved," said Olsen. The case occurred in Tacoma, Washington — a town approximately thirty miles south of Seattle.

"My father is seventy-five years old and lives in Nebraska. Coincidentally, my father is the same age that Charlie Mattson would have been if he had lived. When I told him that I was thinking of writing a book about a case of a doctor's son who was kidnapped and murdered in the 1930s, my dad said, 'You mean the Mattson case?' "

When Olsen's father was growing up in the 1930s, there were no twenty-four-hour-news channels, but somehow the kidnapping and murder of little Charlie Mattson was so far-reaching that people from all corners of the country, and even the world, had heard about it.

"When I asked my father how did he know about the kid, he said, like Charles Lindberg's son, everyone knew about the Mattson's kid kidnapping and murder, and everyone wanted to know about it," Olsen said.

Olsen said that when he recently called Charlie's older brother, who was in the house the night of the kidnapping, the brother had said something very odd to him. "He told me to let sleeping dogs lie and leave the story alone. His attitude really sealed it for me. I knew that there was an outstanding crime story here," he said.

Kidnappings were very prominent during the 1930s. Historically, it seems that every decade is defined by a distinctive crime pattern. Olsen said the 1970s were highly identified with airplane hijacking or "skyjacking" as it came to be known. The 1980s gave rise to financial scams, but the 1930s were defined by high-profile kidnapping.

"Maybe it was because of the Depression, but there were many cases of people kidnapping rich people's children and demanding ransom money," said Olsen. "The kidnapping of Charles Lindberg, Jr. is a classic example." The child was kidnapped from the aviator's home, and tragically, was later found murdered. Olsen said that during that time it seemed that every major city in the country had a high-profile kidnapping case. Washington State seems to have had its share of kidnappings. "In eighteen months five kidnappings, or attempted kidnappings, occurred during the mid-1930s," said Olsen.

"Like with the other books that I have written, the circumstances surrounding Charlie Mattson's death were very compelling," he said. Olsen said Charlie's older brother, who was sixteen, and his sister who was fourteen, were caring for Charlie that evening. Another teenage girl was also at the house visiting at the time. They said a man forced his way into the house, grabbed Charlie and dropped a ransom note demanding $28,000. He said what resulted was a massive investigation. The ransom drop was never made and about twelve days after the kidnapping, Charlie's body was found.

"It was a huge case with President Roosevelt and J. Edgar Hoover getting involved. The FBI took over the investigation and interviewed more than 25,000 people and amassed more than 300,000 pages of material," said Olsen.

## Cold Homicide Cases can be Solved

"Someone has to speak for the dead." That's how Detective Rick Ninomiya describes his job as a "Cold Case" Homicide Detective for the Seattle Police Department. This book focuses on unsolved murders, many occurring years ago, but if Detective Ninomiya has his way, unsolved murders will definitely become a thing of the past.

When homicides are considered unsolvable, detectives usually move on to try to solve the latest crime. The longer the case goes on, in theory, the harder it is to solve. The case then becomes "cold" and goes to the Cold Case Division.

Major police departments across the country have developed cold case divisions, and most are experiencing great success in solving cases that are, in many instances, decades old. In fact, Seattle has an unsolved murder case on the books that dates back to 1907.

There is no statute of limitations on murder, so all murder cases remain officially active until they are technically solved (which means that the killer is eventually brought to trial or there is a summary written with an implication of who the killer is).

"Homicide is the most severe crime you can commit. The victims have rights too, and everybody needs some kind of closure," said Ninomiya. "I remember solving a murder that had happened in 1973. We were able to match fingerprints from the crime scene through the Automated Fingerprint

Identification System (AFIS)." He said the family of the victim had moved to different parts of the country, but most of them came back for the trial. "After twenty-eight years we got a conviction, and I still remember how happy and relieved that family was," said Ninomiya.

That case that stands out so vividly for Ninomiya was the 1973 murder of Gerrit Weynands, a 45-year-old logging business owner who was shot in the back on a Seattle street, his pockets emptied, and his wallet stolen.

He said that Weynands was on a business trip to Seattle and was staying at a hotel. He told one of the employees of the hotel that a prostitute had stolen his wallet the previous night and he was going to meet with someone to bargain for getting it back. He told the employee that the papers in his wallet were important to his business. Weynands was later found dead. Through a meticulous investigation, they were able to build a case against a suspect. New technology was a tremendous help.

A bloody fingerprint was found on Weynands' car, but during the initial investigation, Ninomiya said that even though they had fingerprint evidence, they didn't have a suspect to compare the print against. "There wasn't a system that could check fingerprints extensively," said Ninomiya.

However, in 1996, when an officer was running prints randomly through AFIS, he found a match. It matched the prints of Anthony Lowe, who was then serving a prison sentence on a drug charge.

"At a certain point, time becomes your friend in these investigations," said Ninomiya. "We had to follow up with some good old-fashioned police work in order to build the case."

He said in the Weynands case there was an important witness, but it was a matter of tracking down someone from more than twenty years past. He explained that she lived in a low-cost housing area at the time of the murder. Most of her family that they knew about had either moved or died. The detectives knew she had a three-month-old baby at the time of the murder. They went through King County vital statistics records, and were able to trace her from that.

Ninomiya said again that in some respects, time becomes a positive in solving old murder cases. "As time goes by, people and situations change. People may have developed a conscience, their loyalty to the murderer could have changed, or maybe they are no longer afraid; therefore, they are willing to talk openly now," he said.

Ninomiya and his partner Detective Greg Mixsell are the full-time detectives in Seattle's Cold Case Division. Both are veterans of the force and, in addition to the homicide unit, they have worked in SWAT, robbery, and intelligence divisions, and look forward to tackling the more than 350 unsolved cases on the books.

Ninomiya said developing the Cold Case Division was an arduous task. He visited departments that were up and running and had had success, such as Dade County in Florida, Dallas, and Los Angeles.

"I did a feasibility study and used 1965 as my cut-off date. I calculated that we had hundreds of unsolved cases that, technically, no one was working on," he said.

Seattle's Cold Case Division currently has two full-time detectives, but Ninomiya hopes the division will expand to at least four full time officers.

"You would be surprised by how much information we have to go through; it can be overwhelming," he said.

The Cold Case Division strictly investigates old homicide cases. Mixsell said the Seattle Homicide Unit has a 70 to 80 percent clearance rate (meaning the number of homicides that are solved). Unfortunately, some cases still remain unsolvable because of a lack of evidence.

"I think one of the most disappointing situations is when detectives know who committed the crime, but do not have enough evidence to convict the suspect or even make an arrest," said Ninomiya.

In the fight to close out unsolved cases, technology has been an ally. In addition to AFIS, DNA evidence has been essential in helping to convict perpetrators, and also eliminate some people as well.

"You can get DNA from anything — hair, saliva, chewing gum — whatever," said Ninomiya. "You'd be surprised how much information and evidence we can garner from DNA."

In addition, there is proposed legislation in some states that will require gun manufacturers to document the rifling in each gun that they make. That documentation would then go into a national databank. Both Ninomiya and Mixsell think that if it happens, it would be a great investigative tool and could help homicide investigators tremendously in their job.

"When people are murdered, they leave behind family and friends. These people, as well as the victim, deserve to have the case solved," said Ninomiya.

As to how productive an investigation could be, sometimes, after decades have passed, Ninomiya said, "We're constantly getting tips from people. It could be someone who's charged with one crime, and we want to talk about what he knows on another crime in order to make a deal." Or, he explained, an ex-spouse may decide she doesn't want to keep her ex-husband's secret anymore, or any number of other reasons.

"On inactive homicide cases, if we solve it, we write up a summary and then contact any remaining family," Ninomiya said.

He said that if the killer is still alive, they want to prosecute no matter how many years have passed; however, sometimes the prosecutors' office, for whatever reason, decides not to proceed with the case. At any rate, the detectives can then close the case.

As the Weynands case illustrates, any case, even decades-old cases can be solved, prosecuted, and won at trial.

# Chapter Seven
# The Disappearance
# of Jimmy Hoffa

*Jimmy Hoffa*

Jimmy Hoffa no doubt holds the distinction as the most famous missing person of the twentieth century. The question still remains — how could the very visible, very powerful, former president of one of the most powerful unions in the country disappear in broad daylight without a trace? No one knows what happened to Hoffa, and to this day his body has never been found. There are, of course, theories as to what became of Hoffa's body. One popular theory is that he is buried in the end zone of the Giants football stadium in New Jersey.

What is known is that on July 30, 1975, Hoffa was seen getting into a car in the parking lot of a popular Detroit area restaurant named Manchu's Red Fox, and he was never seen or heard from again.

Before he disappeared, Jimmy Hoffa had fought his way through the ranks to become one of the most powerful union leaders in the country. When Hoffa disappeared, the Teamsters Union boasted well over two million members — making it one of the largest unions in the country.

In 1975, Hoffa was no longer president of the union, but he was trying to make his way back to head the union he loved. There are theories that maybe he was stopped because he had a legitimate chance of achieving that goal.

On the day that he disappeared, Hoffa told his wife that he had a meeting with some people around 2:00 p.m. to resolve the ongoing problems that were preventing him from returning to head the union. He drove his car to the restaurant and waited. Approximately forty-five minutes later he called his wife to ask if anyone had called to cancel because his party hadn't showed up. She told him no one had called and she never heard from him again. Hoffa's car was found in the restaurant parking lot, but there was no trace of him. Hoffa, as a Teamster official, had strong ties to powerful organized crime figures. In fact, those ties made him a special target of an investigative committee looking into ties between the union and organized crime.

## Who was Jimmy Hoffa?

Jimmy Hoffa was born James Riddle Hoffa in the town of Brazil, Indiana, in 1913. Hoffa's father died when he was only seven years old, leaving his mother to raise four children on her own.

A few years after his father's death, the family moved to a working-class neighborhood in Detroit, Michigan. Times were tough and Hoffa ended up quitting school when he was fourteen. He got a job paying $10 a week. The Depression had hit and it was a good salary for the time, but money was still tight for his family.

Soon after, Hoffa landed another job unloading produce from railroad cars for Kroger's, a big grocery chain, making as much as $15 a week. However, Hoffa wasn't satisfied with the way the workers were treated. Their salaries were tied to unreasonable incentives in some cases, so Hoffa and a few others decided to organize. His sense of fairness for workers began at an early age, and by the time he was eighteen years old, Hoffa was instrumental in organizing a union called the International Brotherhood of Teamsters.

The union gave Hoffa a purpose in life. After the success of their first unofficial strike, Hoffa started working for the union full-time, helping among other things, to organize other workers.

Unions were a rough business in the 1930s. Hoffa related in his autobiography that employers would often go to great lengths to not pay their workers a decent wage. Hoffa

claimed that he was attacked many times by thugs that storeowners had hired. He said he fought back hard, using his
fists and his brawn — not his brains. That earned him the
reputation of being a tough guy, which in turn earned him
even more respect from union members.

In 1936, Hoffa met his wife Josephine while both were
marching on a picket line. They were married four months
later. He and his wife had two children — a daughter Bar-
bara, and a son James, who would follow in his father's foot-
steps in the union business. James is currently the national
president of the Teamsters Union.

Hoffa was very adept at union work. He recognized the
need to grow and expand the membership. He realized that
with more members, the more powerful the union would be.
Another important asset of having more members was that
more membership dues that could be collected, and money is
power.

By all accounts, Hoffa's efforts paid off for union members. To this day there are websites devoted to Hoffa, herald-
ing him as a great union leader and organizer. It was the
1930s, during the Depression and Hoffa managed to secure
such benefits for workers as insurance, guaranteed work
schedules and better overall working conditions.

Hoffa was tough and if people crossed picket lines it was
Hoffa who often led the charge in a fight. "Cracking a few
heads" was a necessary part of protecting workers' rights,
reasoned Hoffa. He also recruited brawny "enforcers" to
crack those heads when strikes became physical.

Hoffa's stock in the Union was rising. Union leaders no-
ticed his hard work and they became his strong supporters.
Hoffa also developed other allies along the way — mobsters.
When a rival union faction, the CIO, tried to defect from the
Teamsters, Hoffa was sent to stop the defection. He appar-

ently made a deal with mobsters for additional help in the form of muscle to complete the job. The mobsters held up their part of the deal, and from then on the "Hoffa-mobster" alliance was sealed. One mobster in particular, Anthony Giacolone, became a close friend of Hoffa. Giacolone had been a member of the Detroit mob scene since the 1920s, but that didn't seem to bother Hoffa.

Hoffa had said he didn't judge people by their criminal records, for he himself had had run-ins with the law. For example, he was arrested for extortion on several occasions; one charge resulting from Hoffa being accused of extorting money from storeowners for using non-union drivers. Hoffa appeared to be immune from conviction. The charge was usually pled down, and at most, Hoffa would pay a fine. Despite his arrests, Hoffa's power and respect among union associates continued to rise. His first step to real power came in 1945 when he was elected president of the Detroit Local 299. During that same year he became a member of the Union's Joint Council. The Joint Council oversaw the operations of the entire Detroit area. Being a member of the council put Hoffa in the position of affecting policy for not only his Union hall, but also the entire Detroit area. Hoffa also became the negotiating chairman for the Midwest truckers. Then he began organizing the Southern truck drivers. With his new duties, Hoffa represented well over a half million Teamsters. With the increased membership, the Teamsters' pension and welfare plans totaled in the millions.

Hoffa made a huge mistake, however, by allowing his mob friends to invest the union money. It wasn't long before his most worrisome legal troubles began. Congressional committees looking into mob activity discovered the connection to the now-powerful union boss. Union corruption was in the news and at the center of the controversy was Jimmy Hoffa.

But that didn't seem to matter, because by 1952, Hoffa's power was cemented. At the Teamster's Union National Convention, he was voted in as one of nine vice-presidents.

Power is addicting, and Jimmy Hoffa wanted more of it. He was ambitious and wanted more control at the national level of the union, and apparently he had very few qualms about how he got that power. Allegedly working with a mobster friend, Hoffa rigged a New York Teamsters election. They created local unions on paper, but there were no members. On the strength of those fake votes the election went to Hoffa, which meant that he had control of a powerful state — New York.

A congressional committee looking into labor corruption heard rumors of the New York election and targeted Hoffa in their investigation. Senator McClellan headed the investigation, and that committee's general counsel was Robert Kennedy, who continued his investigation of Hoffa as Attorney General in his brother's, President John F. Kennedy's, administration. Robert Kennedy was relentless in his pursuit of Hoffa, and he kept close tabs on him.

And he provided Kennedy with plenty of ammunition. Hoffa continued to deal with the mob by making questionable "investments" with the union's pension and welfare money. Hoffa was also engaging in questionable, unethical business practices by using his union influence to secure contracts for his private business. In addition, he had been arrested and charged with three felony counts of attempting to bribe a federal official.

The two men developed a hatred for each other. Hoffa managed an acquittal on the bribery charges, but Kennedy seemed determined to nail him in the committee hearings. Hoffa was openly hostile to Kennedy in his answers, sometimes ridiculing Kennedy or not answering the questions at

all. The major complaints against Hoffa were that he personally mishandled union funds, specifically arranging for illegal loans to his friends in the mob. Hoffa again escaped legal
liability through this investigation. Despite his legal woes —
amazingly — the Teamsters Union elected Jimmy Hoffa as
its president in 1957. And as the Teamsters' president, Hoffa
put his legal troubles behind him, worked diligently, and was
a popular and effective leader. He would often work seven
days a week. He was probably so well-liked by the membership because he constantly flew across the country visiting as
many locals as he possibly could. If there was a strike called,
as president, Hoffa was there, walking the picket lines shoulder to shoulder with the members. He was also an excellent
negotiator — nearly always securing contracts that were
overwhelmingly in favor of the Teamsters.

The Teamsters Union was a union mired in corruption —
many of its top officials were either indicted or on their way
to jail. Hoffa, either because he wasn't aware of, or maybe
because he was heavily involved in the corruption himself,
turned a blind eye to what was going on. It's highly doubtful
that Hoffa wasn't aware of the activities, because he prided
himself on knowing almost everything that was union-
related.

Hoffa again eluded prosecution, a situation not lost on
Robert Kennedy. Kennedy had his own critics. There were
those who believed that Kennedy had brought his personal
animosity toward Hoffa into the legal arena. Kennedy recon-
vened the investigative committee and set out for another
round with Jimmy Hoffa. Again, Hoffa managed to escape
unscathed.

By 1961, however, some of the rank-and-file members
were becoming disenchanted with Hoffa's tactics and the
rumored corruption. But they realized that going up against

the powerful union leader would lead them nowhere, so it was business as usual. Hoffa was elected president again. He probably would have won anyway, but during the election process, he didn't allow any other nominations to be heard. Hoffa added to his problems by allowing convicted felons to be part of the union, despite rumblings from some members and it being against the union bylaws. Union money was even used to defend these men some of whom were charged with new felonies.

Hoffa's relationship with the mob continued. Some mob figures became new members of the Union, and they were being placed in key positions. Union money also continued to be used by the mob. One member, who was reportedly a high-ranking figure in the New York mob, with Hoffa's aid, actually ascended to a position of vice-president.

In 1961, John F. Kennedy was elected President. Robert Kennedy became Attorney General, and he went back to investigating Hoffa. Kennedy had been keeping track of Hoffa's numerous arrests. In 1962, Hoffa's legal problems intensified, and he was brought to trial for extortion. Even though the jury acquitted Hoffa on the extortion charge, a subsequent investigation was launched, looking into the possibility of jury tampering.

In 1963, Hoffa was charged with jury tampering and indicted on charges of mishandling the Union pension fund. On the jury tampering indictment, Hoffa was charged with bribing several jurors who served on his extortion trial.

The fraud charges included making illegal loans (presumably to the mob), and approving unsecured loans. Hoffa laid his legal problems squarely at the feet of Robert Kennedy. His hatred of the Kennedys knew no bounds. When President Kennedy was assassinated, Hoffa was quoted as saying "Good — he deserved it." But if Hoffa thought that his brother's death would distract Robert Kennedy, he was wrong. The Attorney General seemed more determined than ever to finish what he had started and secure a conviction against Hoffa.

Hoffa had grown confident of receiving acquittals, so he wasn't worried about the jury tampering trial. In 1964, his trial got underway. His defense team was blindsided by a witness who said he had first-hand knowledge of Hoffa's jury tampering. Edward Partin, a union boss out of Louisiana, testified that Hoffa had personally asked him to deliver a large sum of money to several jurors.

Partin said he had been loyal to Hoffa, but the boss' behavior had become increasingly out of control over the years, and he and other union members thought he had to be stopped. Partin went on to explain how Hoffa often quieted those members who voiced opposition to him — they or their families were often threatened or beaten into submission.

The defense tried to impeach Partin's testimony by bringing out the fact that he had a criminal past (as did a lot of the Teamsters members). It didn't work. His testimony was so compelling that the jury concluded that he was telling the truth and found Hoffa guilty of the jury tampering and fraud charges. Hoffa was sentenced to eight years in prison and a $150,000 fine. To make matters worse for the Teamsters' leader, he was also found guilty in a later trial of mishandling the union pension fund. That crime also carried a lengthy prison sentence.

Hoffa's defense, of course, appealed the verdicts, but after three years Hoffa had to face the inevitable. In 1967, Hoffa began serving his sentence at the federal penitentiary in Lewisburg, Pennsylvania.

To Hoffa's credit, he adjusted to prison life very well. He was a favorite among other inmates. He helped them organize and bargain for better living conditions. He also kept busy by working out and meeting with his attorneys. And he kept his hand in union business from prison; he didn't resign from being president.

Hoffa had hand-picked an old friend, Frank Fitzsimmons, to be General Vice President. Fitzsimmons had been a loyal Hoffa supporter and assured Hoffa that once he got out, he would once again be top man, and he would graciously step aside.

However, Fitzsimmons had plans of his own. Power is as addictive as any drug, and once Fitzsimmons got a taste of it, he wasn't eager to let it go. He stopped communicating with Hoffa in prison and started to make union business decisions on his own.

Fitzsimmons was now the person who commanded the membership, and who traveled all over the country negotiating contracts, making deals, and being quoted in the media. Hoffa was helpless to stop Fitzsimmons. The man he had trusted was now running the union without Hoffa's counsel or advice. Hoffa held many key positions within the union other than president. He held key leadership positions in various locals, especially in major states, and on national boards. In fact, many union members had complained that when Hoffa was in charge he ran a one-man show — rarely sharing his power with anyone. Fitzsimmons' ascendancy to power suited some just fine. Hoffa often worked as much as eighteen hours a day, seven days a week and that schedule didn't appeal to Fitzsimmons. He wasn't as shrewd as Hoffa and people took advantage of that. Hoffa was infuriated that so many had control of the union business reins, and worked with his lawyers constantly trying to overturn his conviction.

When the appeals process had been exhausted, Hoffa realized there was only one way out — through parole. So, he decided to resign from the presidency, thinking it might give him a better opportunity to receive parole.

At the 1971 convention, Frank Fitzsimmons was elected President of the Teamsters Union. He and Hoffa also had something else in common — Fitzsimmons, too, had close connections with the mob. Fitzsimmons, as if following Hoffa's odyssey, also recommended high-ranking union positions to leading crime figures. He also made large, unsecured loans to mobsters out of the pension fund.

Fitzsimmons, in many respects, proved to be even worse than Hoffa. Where the union was Hoffa's life, Fitzsimmons seemed to think first and foremost of his personal wealth. He allegedly received large kickbacks from the loans he made. Where Hoffa engaged in risky loans and business dealings with the mob, Fitzsimmons opened the coffers completely. He also wasn't as popular with the rank and file as Hoffa was. In an effort to try to appease some of the most vocal Hoffa supporters, Fitzsimmons, after assuring that Hoffa could no longer run as Union President, struck a deal with Richard Nixon. If Nixon pardoned Hoffa, Fitzsimmons promised him that the Teamsters would endorse him in the next election.

The deal was done, and in 1971, Jimmy Hoffa was pardoned by President Nixon and left prison with the stipulation that he was precluded from any Teamsters Union business for at least ten years. Once free, Hoffa claimed that when he signed the pardon there was no such provision in the agreement.

Hoffa returned to Michigan and continued to fight the clause in his pardon until the time of his disappearance. If his past venom had been directed toward Robert Kennedy in the heyday of their battles, that venom was now directed toward Frank Fitzsimmons. Hoffa went public, telling the media of the connection between Fitzsimmons and the mob. He made allegations that Fitzsimmons had also mishandled union funds — the same charge that he was eventually found guilty of. In typical old union fashion, the confrontations between Hoffa's and Fitzsimmons' supporters grew violent.

While they each had their supporters, one mob member who was squarely in Fitzsimmons' corner was Tony Provenzano. The two had been long-time friends and associates. Provenzano was a high-ranking member of the Genovese crime family in New York. He had headed up the New Jersey local union before being sent to jail for extortion.

With Hoffa out of the picture, the mob could easily manipulate Fitzsimmons, and have even more access to the union's money. Hoffa was still very popular with the rank and file, and if he got the restriction lifted from his pardon, there was a very real chance that he could win the election for union president again.

On the day that he disappeared, Hoffa told his wife that he had a late luncheon meeting to talk about union business, but she didn't know with whom. Manchu's Red Fox restaurant was a short drive from Hoffa's home. He was expected back home later that afternoon.

His wife was worried when he didn't return home that afternoon. When Hoffa didn't return home by the following morning, his wife called the police. They found his car in the parking lot of the restaurant. The car had not been broken into nor did it show any signs of being tampered with. Also, the police found no evidence of foul play, such as blood.

Federal authorities believed that mob bosses murdered Hoffa because he wanted the Teamsters Union presidency back — and given Hoffa's tenacity and ambition, he could have achieved that goal. "But the evidence is not there for conviction," one investigator was quoted as saying.

According to an article written in the *Detroit News* and reprinted on a website, Hoffa had threatened to expose the connections and dealings between the mob and the union by providing documentation and giving details about unsecured loans that Fitzsimmons had given crime figures, loans that totaled in the millions from the union pension fund.

The article went on to say, "investigators believed that Hoffa was to meet Provenzano the day he disappeared. There is no proof the two ever met — but investigators said Provenzano had a clear message for Hoffa: "Get out of union politics, or else."

## Who are the Suspects?

According to a newspaper series done in the *Detroit Sunday Journal* and reprinted on a website titled *The Hoffa Files*, these are the major suspects in Hoffa's disappearance:

**Tony Provenzano** — who had been a union official with the local New Jersey Teamsters and a high-ranking member of the Genovese crime family. Although he and Hoffa had shared a close friendship dating back years, animosity grew between the two when they were both at the penitentiary in Lewisburg. While there Hoffa supposedly struck up a friendship with someone from a rival New York crime family.

Provenzano had always denied that he was in any way responsible for Hoffa's disappearance, and denied he had any meeting plans with Hoffa that day. He died in prison in 1988, while serving a twenty-year sentence for labor racketeering.

Provenzano had an alibi the day Hoffa disappeared. He said he was playing cards at his former teamster hall in New

Jersey. The FBI, who had launched an extensive investigation, confirmed Provenzano's story. There were many witnesses who confirmed they saw him in New Jersey.

**Chuckie O'Brien** — was a loyal Hoffa supporter who had practically grown up in Hoffa's house as a child. Hoffa often referred to him as his adopted son, but O'Brien had turned his support to Fitzsimmons. He had also become very close to crime boss Tony Giacalone. At the time of Hoffa's disappearance, O'Brien said he was at an athletic club in Detroit, but the club's records didn't show he was there. According to the newspaper series, authorities believe it was O'Brien who was actually driving the car that Hoffa was seen entering that fateful day. Authorities believe Hoffa thought he was meeting both Provenzano and Tony Giacalone to come to terms on their differences.

When a federal grand jury convened later that year and called O'Brien, he invoked his Fifth Amendment privilege on all questions relating to Jimmy Hoffa.

The article stated that investigators theorize that Hoffa was waiting at the restaurant, O'Brien drove up and told him that the meeting place had been changed, and said he would take Hoffa there. Hoffa then got out of his car and got into the car with O'Brien. Even though they were estranged, some believe Hoffa never thought that his "adopted son" would participate in his murder. Most believe that O'Brien probably didn't know that Hoffa was going to be killed when he was asked to drive. The assassins were probably sitting in the back seat or waiting at a predetermined place and Hoffa was instantly killed. O'Brien was then threatened with death if he didn't keep his mouth shut.

**Frank Fitzsimmons** — who some believe was a hand puppet for the mob, enjoyed his position of power. He realized that Hoffa could legitimately challenge him for the Union presidency and could cause all kinds of legal problems for him.

Fitzsimmons died of lung cancer in 1981.

**Tony Giacalone** — was a member of a Detroit crime family. He, like Provenzano, had been a close friend of Hoffa's, but their relationship had soured. Giacalone was also a close friend of O'Brien and his family. It was Giacalone that many believe contacted Hoffa and offered that he, Hoffa, and Provenzano meet to discuss matters.

He denied any involvement and provided an alibi. He said he was at the Southfield Athletic Club (the same club O'Brien said he had been) getting a massage. Records and witnesses showed that he was actually at the club.

He was sentenced to prison after Hoffa's disappearance for tax evasion.

**Joseph Giacalone** — was the son of Tony Giacalone. He and Chuckie O'Brien were very good friends, and authorities confirmed that it was his car that O'Brien borrowed that day to pick up Hoffa from the restaurant. According to the newspaper series, the FBI found trace evidence of Hoffa's hair in the back seat, but without other corroborating evidence, they couldn't determine when the hair was left there.

# Chapter Eight
# Who Killed
# Kenneth Rex McElroy?

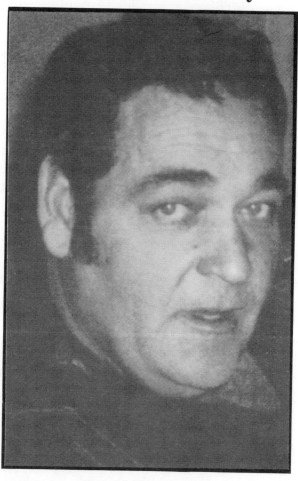

*Kenneth Rex McElroy*

When you think of a bully, it usually takes you back to your elementary school days. Rarely do bullies continue to torture people well into adulthood. Unfortunately, in the town of Skidmore, Missouri, the townspeople were faced with just that kind of bully.

Kenneth Rex McElroy ran roughshod over the entire town, threatening anyone who stood in his way — and he usually enforced those threats with physical violence. According to the A&E program, *Skidmore: Frontier Justice*, McElroy's reign of terror had included burning down a house, rape, shooting several men, and regularly and forcefully beating up on "his women." He threatened to kill anyone who pressed charges or testified against him in court. People in the town learned, often the hard way, that he meant his threats, so they usually withdrew their complaints; therefore, he always eluded conviction and was free to continue to terrorize the people of Skidmore.

The people in the town didn't think the law would ever punish McElroy, so they decided to take matters into their own hands. On July 10, 1981, McElroy was sitting in his truck in front of a tavern on Elm Street (the main street in town). He had started the engine of his pickup truck when men on the street started walking toward the truck. Even more men begin to come out of the tavern heading towards the truck. It was only 10:30 a.m., and McElroy had already been drinking. The men had looks of determination on their faces. McElroy's wife, Trena, was sitting next to him in the truck. She was frightened, and, as it turned out, she had every right to be. Two guns from different directions were fired. The rear window of the truck shattered and according to newspaper accounts, one shot tore through McElroy's face — ripping open his tongue, and tearing out teeth and bone fragments. The bullet was from a 30/30-caliber rifle. Another gun fired, a .22-caliber rifle, which the medical examiner later concluded was the shot that killed McElroy. That bullet entered McElroy's head, shattering his skull. He slumped over — dead.

McElroy's reign of terror was finally over. He had been killed in broad daylight in the middle of town in front of more than forty witnesses and no one was talking. They all said they didn't know who killed the man, but all said he deserved his fate.

Skidmore is a quiet farm community. It may seem like a town of long ago. An A&E *City Confidential* television special detailing the events described Skidmore as a town that was home to such quaint pleasures as harvest celebrations, a squash festival, and square dancing. The people are law-abiding, hardworking, and upstanding. Although it was a farm community, most of the farmers did quite well. They loved their town and their way of life. They had escaped the hustle and bustle of city life. During the year that McElroy was killed, the town had no movie theaters, no traffic lights, and only one restaurant — but the people seemed to have everything that they needed. There was a larger town a mere twenty miles away where people could get those things. Life would have been idyllic if it wasn't for one major problem, and his name was Kenneth Rex McElroy — Ken Rex as he was called.

## Who was Ken McElroy?

What makes a person a bully? It's hard to say. McElroy's childhood was not a bed of roses, but that holds true for a lot of people. McElroy was born into a poor family, and was the thirteenth of fourteen children in his family. He grew up in Skidmore after his family finally settled there and bought a farm, after moving from town to town, constantly following his father, who had worked at many jobs.

He was mean and hot-tempered even as a child — and was a bully very early in his life. He was bigger than most of the children in his classes, partly due to the fact that he had been held back so much. He seemed to revel in pushing around his schoolmates, doing everything it took to get his way. Predictably, he was a failure at school. When he was fourteen or fifteen he could barely read or write, and finally gave up on school and quit. He was only in the sixth grade.

McElroy tried farming on his family's place, but he wasn't cut out for it. He had been at odds with the law since he was thirteen. From early on in his life, he stole from his neighbors without remorse or regard to what hardships his thievery put them in. There were rarely any eyewitnesses, and law enforcement officers were helpless to do anything. They couldn't arrest him without evidence or witnesses, and McElroy was smart enough not to leave evidence and he avoided witnesses.

By the time he was eighteen years old he seemed to have found his niche in life — training coonhounds for sale. It could have been a profitable profession if he had pursued it, but McElroy always seemed to revert to the easy way out — stealing. He had become a modern day rustler, stealing people's livestock (hogs, cattle, or horses). Rustling seemed to have provided him with a comfortable living. He sold the animals to markets or at auctions.

At eighteen, McElroy got married. He and his wife moved briefly to Colorado where he worked in construction. McElroy got hurt on the job, sustaining a head injury, and they soon returned to Missouri.

When he returned to Skidmore, he resumed his thieving ways. His impunity from the law was established early on.

During one of his rustling capers, a farmer caught him stealing two of his horses. The man filed charges against McElroy. This infuriated Ken Rex. When he went over to the man's house to convince him to withdraw his complaint, he took along his rifle. When the man refused, he savagely beat him with the rifle, and threatened that the next time would be even worse. After that incident, the farmer dropped the charges.

McElroy also terrorized the town in another way — by having his way with as many women as he could. Their ages or marital status seemed irrelevant to him. As a matter of fact, young girls seemed to be his specialty. In his book *In Broad Daylight*, Harry MacLean chronicles McElroy's list of young women. He had a sexual affair with a girl who was thirteen years old. The girl lived with her grandparents and when her grandfather tried to put a stop to it, McElroy threatened to burn the man's house down. Ken-Rex was married, in his mid-twenties, and he got the girl pregnant. He lost interest in the young girl not because of the law or her grandfather, but because of her pregnancy.

McElroy wanted what he wanted and he used violence to achieve it. Another of his "love" interests — a fifteen-year-old named Sharon soon learned that fact the hard way, when an argument turned extremely violent. McElroy took out his rifle and shot her in the face. The bullet hit her in the chin and left a prominent, permanent scar. Amazingly, despite being shot by her lover, Sharon married McElroy after he and his first wife divorced. Sharon had four children with McElroy and throughout their marriage he beat her unmercifully. Not one to settle for just one woman, he soon set his eyes on a 13-year-old named Sally. He moved Sally into his family's farmhouse where his parents still lived. Sally bore him three children. McElroy, in all his boldness, even moved Sharon and her children to the farm with Sally still there.

However, his attention wandered again and he spent little time at the farm because he had a new girlfriend, an eighteen-year-old named Alice. He was spending most of his time at the eighteen-year-old's apartment.

The other two women eventually moved out of his farmhouse and Alice moved in. Alice also endured beatings and mistreatment from McElroy, and had a son with him.

McElroy continued to steal. After a rash of burglaries in another county, the sheriff suspected that McElroy was behind the thefts, but proving it was another matter. Finally, the sheriff got a break.

Maybe to please McElroy or to lessen her beatings, Alice sometimes helped with his burglaries. She was stopped one day by the sheriff, while carrying some of the stolen merchandise. She finally broke down and confessed, implicating McElroy, who was charged with burglary.

Ken-Rex hired a lawyer who succeeded in obtaining a number of lengthy continuances. By the time (almost a year after he had been charged) Alice was to give her deposition, she had changed her story. McElroy liked his lawyer's style, so Richard McFadin from Kansas City became his permanent attorney, and his client provided McFadin with plenty of work.

As expected with a man like McElroy, he succumbed to all of his urges, whether it was bullying, beating women or drinking — and he drank a lot. When he drank, he grew even meaner. Alice had grown tired of the bad treatment, left her husband and moved to her grandparents' home. However, whatever joy she experienced from leaving McElroy was short-lived, for unlike Sharon and Sally, he wasn't ready to let Alice leave. He hunted her down and threatened her grandfather. When the old man refused to throw out his granddaughter and great-grandson, McElroy showed up at the man's house with his rifle. One night he drove over, shot out the window, and a bullet lodged in the man's leg. McElroy was charged with assault. The case hinged on one witness — Alice's grandfather, Othe Embrey.

McElroy was always adamant that he wasn't going to jail, and he set about making sure that didn't happen. The sure-fire method of achieving that was by intimidating Embrey — and he did it with a vengeance. He constantly harassed Embrey — following him in his car, phoning his house and threatening to kill him or his wife. He even cornered the old man in a bar and shot at him, but missed.

McFadin was able to get the trial delayed and Embrey grew tired of the threats against him and his wife — so he refused to testify and the charges were dropped. McElroy was free to terrorize again. Beaten down, Alice returned to him.

Soon, however, another girl entered the picture. She was only twelve years old when McElroy set his sights on Trena McCloud. He made no secret of the fact that he was having sex with the young girl. By the time she was fourteen she was pregnant with McElroy's baby and had a son. She moved to the farm with him and Alice and her son.

Even though McElroy was almost forty, his disposition towards his women hadn't softened. Trena soon learned the brutal reality of living with Ken McElroy. He resorted to beating her (as he continued to do with Alice) and forcing her into savage sex acts. Trena had dropped out of school when she was only twelve years old, her family was poor, and she was trapped.

The women had grown tired of the beatings and had tried to run away at one point. They had taken their children and moved to a relative of Trena's. One night the women were riding around in Trena's stepfather's car when McElroy found them and forced them back to the farm, where both were severely beaten and forced to have sex with him. For the stepfather's part in interfering with his women, he went over to the man's house with a can of gasoline, doused the house, set it on fire and burned it down.

Trena's injuries from the beating were severe enough that she needed to see a doctor. The doctor notified authorities, and McElroy was charged with assault and rape (Trena, at that time was still a minor). She was also placed in foster care.

However, it appeared the law again couldn't touch McElroy. He continually harassed her and her foster mother. He engaged in his patented form of harassment — driving by the house, parking across the street, or brandishing his rifle.

Trena gave up and, astonishingly, she went back to McElroy, but refused to testify against him in court. To be sure she didn't change her mind, McElroy divorced Sharon and married Trena in 1974.

## What Finally Set the Town Off?

Bo and Lois Bowenkamp owned the local store in Skidmore. Bo was almost seventy, and Lois was younger, in her late forties. They were strong, proud people and like most of the people in town, they had had enough of McElroy, his brutality and his seemingly constant pass from the law. According to the A&E special, the events that led to McElroy's death started in April, 1980, when two of McElroy's children came into the store. One was a teenage daughter from an earlier marriage, the other Trena's daughter, who was pre-school age. When they were leaving, the younger girl took some candy. When the store clerk called their attention to the fact that they hadn't paid for the candy, they got angry and stormed out of the store.

Later that day, another one of Ken Rex's teenage daughters showed up and cursed the clerk for accusing her half-sister of stealing. (Some of McElroy's children from the many women he had previous sexual encounters with lived with him.) She demanded an apology. However, the clerk stood by her accusation and wouldn't back down. After that daughter left, McElroy and Trena showed up. He reportedly remained silent as Trena cursed the clerk and Lois, also demanding an apology for her family.

Lois, a feisty woman, had heard enough and told the McElroys that she didn't want their business anymore. McElroy, now in his mid-forties, wasn't going to let anyone get away with talking to him like that. It outraged him that anyone would accuse his children of stealing. He was still an imposing man — he was 5'10" tall and he weighed almost 250 pounds. His face was etched in meanness.

He embarked on his campaign of terror of the Bowenkamps. That same night he and Trena drove slowly by the Bowenkamps' house in different trucks, making sure to make enough noise so that Bo and Lois knew they were there. A few days later, he and Trena engaged in the same activity — driving by, then leaving — only to return and park for long periods. When he saw Bo on the street, he made disparaging remarks about Lois. Bo mostly ignored Ken Rex, but that only fueled his anger.

A few weeks later Ken Rex and Trena drove to the Bowenkamps' house, parked, got his shotgun and fired towards the house — missing it. A few days later he returned to repeat the scene. Lois called the town's sheriff. But when Ken Rex was questioned, he said he wasn't there and even provided a host of alibi witnesses. There was nothing the sheriff could do.

As the summer continued, McElroy kept up his harassment of the Bowenkamps. The sequence of events that led up to his death was set in motion on July 8, 1980. Bo Bowenkamp was standing at the back dock of his store late that evening waiting for a delivery. McElroy had been drinking at the tavern most of the day. When he left the tavern, he spotted Bowenkamp and headed over to confront him. After a heated exchange of words, Bowenkamp walked into the back of his store; McElroy took his rifle from the rack on his truck and shot Bowenkamp in the neck. People at the tavern heard the commotion, rushed over and someone called the police and an ambulance. When the police arrived Bowenkamp told them what happened and who shot him — Ken Rex McElroy. The police charged McElroy with felony assault. He posted the bail and was out on the streets of Skidmore again.

McElroy thought he would handle this altercation with the law the same way that he always did — by intimidating witnesses. He made it known to everyone in town that anyone who stood beside the Bowenkamps stood against him, a stance that could prove to be dangerous. He threatened everyone whom he thought would testify against him, including the sheriff who arrested him. McElroy confronted the sheriff on a street one day. He demanded to know if he was going to testify against him. When the sheriff said yes, he leveled his rifle directly at the sheriff's head. The Sheriff walked away — but resigned soon afterwards.

Finally, the preliminary hearing took place. Ken Rex's lawyer was skillful as always. McFadin argued that Bo Bowenkamp tried to attack McElroy with a butcher's knife and McElroy was only acting in self-defense. Bowenkamp ad-

---

mitted that when he saw McElroy parked outside of his store, and after their argument, he did pick up the knife for protection. The judge bound McElroy over for trial.

McFadin embarked on a number of maneuvers to delay the trial. He asked for a change of venue, arguing that McElroy couldn't get a fair trial in that county. The judge granted him his change of venue motion. In all, McFadin was able to stall the trial date for more than a year, giving McElroy plenty of time to pressure the Bowenkamps, and any one else who was openly supportive of the Bowenkamps. He called them up and threatened to kill them, their wives, and their children; the man knew no boundaries. As for Bo Bowenkamp, McElroy had a clear message: testify and die.

But the town had grown tired of McElroy. He wasn't the force that he once was. In 1980 he was forty-seven years old and from all of the alcohol abuse he had grown fat, slow and maybe a little vulnerable. The townspeople had noticed something else — unlike in earlier years, he wasn't following up on his threats with action.

The trial finally got underway in another town on June 2, 1981. His attorney used the self-defense angle. McElroy even took the stand, saying that Bo Bowenkamp came after him with a knife and he shot at him only to protect himself. Ken Rex's testimony didn't sway the jury as they convicted him of assault — a crime that carried five years in prison. McFadin immediately filed for an appeal, which meant that McElroy was free on bond pending that appeal.

Within a week he was in the tavern waving an M-1 rifle with a bayonet attached and describing in detail what he intended to do to Bowenkamp. He was prohibited from carrying a gun while his case was on appeal and people in the bar knew it, and one of them reported the incident to the authorities. Finally, the citizens thought that the law was working against McElroy for a change because the prosecutor filed a petition to have his bond revoked based on the gun violation and a hearing was set for July 10.

Thanks to McFadin the hearing was postponed, and McElroy began threatening people again. But something had changed, people no longer averted their eyes when they passed him on the street, they even glared in disgust at him. They weren't afraid of him anymore.

Some men of the town decided they needed to take action — after all, a united front was a strong front. They wanted to protect Bo Bowenkamp and they reasoned if they stood together helping each other out, McElroy couldn't take them all on. According to A&E, they devised a plan. If McElroy came by one person's house to start his reign of intimidation, someone would call to alert other people of the town and they would come over to protect that person. They had noticed that McElroy was less likely to attack a whole group.

Something had to be done, and some of the men held a meeting at the town's American Legion Hall. Many reporters have tried to find out what was discussed, in the meeting. If a plan to kill McElroy was discussed no one has ever said.

Ken Rex decided to go into town the morning of July 10. He must have known that he was no longer a towering force, but he went with Trena. He was sitting at the bar having a beer when word spread that he was in town. The men at the Legion Hall decided to head over to the bar. Once there, they surrounded Ken Rex, staring him down as he had done to them so many times. Perhaps McElroy was intimidated by the show of unity. Like so many bullies, pushing around someone who is smaller or weaker is one thing, but facing a crowd of people who evidently won't be bullied is quite another. Or maybe he just didn't want to face most of the town at once. For whatever reasons, only a few minutes after the crowd arrived, he told Trena they were leaving. When they came out of the bar, men started to come out into the street. They were in his truck when Trena claimed that she saw Del Clement, the owner of the tavern, take his rifle out of his truck and the shooting started. She admitted that she didn't actually see him pull the trigger, but she was convinced that he was one of the shooters. Trena managed to escape from the truck into a nearby building.

When the police arrived about a half-hour later, only a few people were left on the street. The crowd had disappeared. The medic unit had arrived and announced that Kenneth Rex McElroy was dead.

There will always be the question of, how did the situation get this far with Kenneth Rex McElroy? The local authorities, not wanting to have a conflict of interest, turned the case over to state authorities. A task force was eventually established that included police officers from outside the town of Skidmore. During their investigation they talked with Del Clement, who said he didn't shoot McElroy and that he didn't know who did, but he wasn't sorry that the man was dead. Every single person that was interviewed repeated Clement's account — no one saw who did it and no one was sorry that McElroy was dead. Investigators heard many stories of McElroy's brutality, but as to who killed him, they couldn't come up with a single lead. After less than a month, they wrapped up the case and left town.

After the task force concluded their investigation, local authorities convened a grand jury to conduct their own inquiry. All of the witnesses again testified under oath that they didn't see anything and that they didn't know who killed McElroy. Most of those interviewed claimed that when they heard shots they hid under cars or under tables in the bar. Again, no arrest could be made, because of lack of evidence.

There were numerous other investigations, even one conducted by the FBI, but the result was always the same.

The Kenneth McElroy story, to the amazement of the Skidmore community, became national news. Reporters and television producers descended upon the town, hoping to solve the case. But all they got was the same response that the special task force, the local police, and the FBI got — no one saw anything, no one knew who killed McElroy, and, more importantly, no one cared who did.

Is it possible that when the bullets started flying everyone hit the pavement in fear and no one actually saw anything? That scenario is highly unlikely, but to this day the people of Skidmore have kept their secret.

Even though her husband horribly abused Trena, she grieved over his death. She told anyone who would listen that her husband's murder was being ignored by authorities, and that he was murdered simply because the people in town didn't like him (an understatement to say the least). She testified in all of the grand juries and investigations saying that Clement was the man who killed her husband. With the help of McFadin she filled a wrongful death suit against the town, the police, and Del Clement. Since her claim could not be corroborated, the case was not successful. She eventually left Skidmore.

McElroy was the closest that he had ever been to going to jail when he was killed. The biggest question that remains, is why did McElroy practically force a confrontation with the townspeople? In a newspaper article, an acquaintance of his had said that McElroy was adamant about one thing — he wasn't going to jail.

# Chapter Nine
# The Hunt for
# the Green River Killer

From 1982 through 1990, forty-nine young women were found murdered in and around the Seattle, Washington, area — all victims of one man, a serial killer. He was dubbed the "Green River Killer," because the first victims' bodies had been dumped along the riverbank. The murders launched one of the largest investigations in the history of criminal justice.

The Green River is an expansive river that runs for several miles, starting from Mount Rainier, one of Washington State's highest mountains, and moving through several cities until finally winding down near Seattle.

Seattle is nicknamed "the Emerald City," and it's a beautiful city that has the perfect balance between a major metropolis with a small-town atmosphere. But there are big city aspects to the area. It was home to not only the Green River Killer, but also one of the most famous serial killers in the country — Ted Bundy.

David Reichert, now Sheriff of King County, Washington (the largest county in Washington State and includes the city of Seattle), was a detective with the Major Crimes Squad in 1982 when the killings started. Reichert was considered one of the department's brightest and best officers. Even after all these years Reichert remembers vividly most of the names of the victims, the circumstances of their deaths, and the dates their bodies were found.

*Sheriff David Reichert*
*King County, Washington*

In August, 1982, Reichert got a call at home that someone had found a woman's nude body floating face down along the riverbank. "She was nude, and her body was pretty well sun-baked — it was a nasty scene," Reichert said, describing what he discovered.

Even before he had received the coroner's report, Reichert said he knew the woman had been murdered. One of the officers at the scene was from the neighboring city of Kent, Washington, and he told Reichert about a murdered woman's nude body that their department had discovered only a couple of weeks earlier. On July Fifteenth, two boys had found the body along the riverbank. When the Kent police arrived they discovered that the young woman had a pair of jeans tied tightly around her neck. She was identified as Wendy Coffield, a sixteen-year-old prostitute. The medical examiner ruled that her death was due to ligature strangulation.

When Reichert returned to his desk, he compared any similarities that he could find between Wendy Coffield's death and this new victim. Initially, he didn't think there were enough similarities to cause concern, but there were enough to make him want to investigate further. Both women were young and white. Reichert said he studied some case files of unsolved murders for the last few months and discovered that Leann Wilcox was another young woman whose nude body had been found along the Green River a few months earlier. She was also a prostitute, and she had been strangled. Reichert thought if the latest victim was also a prostitute, there was a definite possibility that the three murders were connected.

Reichert sent the latest victim's fingerprints through to the State Crime Lab and she was identified as Deborah Lynn Bonner — a twenty-three-year-old prostitute. Bonner had been convicted of prostitution several times, and she had gone by an alias.

"Before we had the technology and procedures that we do now, a lot of the women who worked as prostitutes used different names when they were arrested. With a different name, they would show up in the system as first-time offenders and get probation or a fine," said Reichert.

He said he then had to do the toughest part of a police officer's job — go out and inform Bonner's parents that their daughter was dead. Her parents, of course, were devastated at the news, and they told Reichert that they had been worried since their daughter had disappeared three weeks earlier because she was frightened for her life. She had asked her parents to help raise bail money for her boyfriend, Carl Martin. They then showed Reichert a note written by a family friend, a bartender, saying that Martin owed a great deal of money to a man named Larry Mathews. The money was owed as the result of a drug deal. If the money wasn't paid, the note continued, Martin would be killed. According to a newspaper article, the bartender said that Deborah Bonner had told him that she was terrified of Mathews and thought he was following her. The last the Bonners knew, Debbie and her boyfriend had left the area. Reichert thought that he had found a good lead on Bonner's death and had put the possible connection of the three murders on hold.

On August 15, Reichert got a call from a patrol officer who informed him that a man out rafting had found two more nude bodies of young women along the riverbank. Reichert went to the scene, and found that both victims were black. Both bodies were weighed down with rocks, an obvious attempt to keep them from being found too quickly.

When the medical examiner arrived, he did a preliminary examination at the scene. He concluded that the first woman was in her early twenties and had been in the water for several days. She was completely nude. The second woman had been in the water for more than a week and she showed signs of decomposition. She was also nude, except for a bra that was unfastened and revealed her breasts.

Reichert walked along the riverbank, looking for evidence and trying to follow the killer's trail, and said he almost tripped over a third body. She was also black and was nude from the waist down. She, too, wore a bra that was unfastened and, as reminiscent of Wendy Coffield's body, she had her jeans tied around her neck. The Medical Examiner determined that victim number three had been dead for twenty-four hours — rigor mortis had set in.

Reichert thought that the killer or killers used a boat to dump the bodies because the riverbank was very steep, making it unlikely that the bodies were carried to the dumping site.

Seattle was the home to one of the most famous serial killers in the country — Ted Bundy. Major Richard Kraske, who at the time was the head of the Criminal Investigation Unit, had been the lead investigator in the Ted Bundy case. The thought that there may be another serial killer was discouraging. Kraske didn't want to go through the pains of another long, drawn-out serial killing investigation.

Ted Bundy was tried and convicted of murdering three young women (one only twelve years old) and he was accused of murdering at least twenty-five more, eight in the Seattle area. Bundy continued his spree to such states as Utah and Colorado before finally stopping in Florida. He was executed by the state of Florida in 1989.

Reichert was present for the examination of these latest three victims. The victim that Reichert had found had sperm in her vagina. He supervised as all three victims' fingerprints were taken and their teeth x-rayed to help in the identification. The second victim had an odd-shaped rock inserted in her vagina and she had probably been strangled. The third victim also had a similar shaped rock inserted into her vagina. The bruising on her neck also indicated that she had been strangled.

When Reichert took the fingerprints to be analyzed, he was able to identify only one of the victims. Her name was Marcia Chapman. Chapman was also a prostitute and had been arrested under various aliases.

"It was a big surprise, of course, finding three bodies," said Reichert.

The fact that this victim was also a prostitute was disturbing to both Reichert and Kraske. They realized that a pattern was developing and more than likely they had one killer on the loose.

They wasted little time in trying to get a handle on the case. Reichert continued to follow up on the identification of the victims, and they set up what Reichert describes as a proactive squad of detectives to investigate the murders. The squad consisted of officers who had specialized skills. Along with Reichert, the squad included then-Detective Fae Brooks from the Sex Crimes Unit, Detective Larry Gross from the Warrants Section, Detectives Pat Ferguson and Ben Caldwell, both very experienced investigators, and Liz Druin, who was a great administrator.

"One of the frustrations of the case was trying to identify the victims," said Fae Brooks, who is now Chief of the Major Crimes Unit of the King County Sheriff's office. "It was common practice for prostitutes to use different names when they were arrested. In some cases that's what took so long to discover that some of the women were missing or to identify them by their correct name."

*Chief Fae Brooks*
*Chief of the Major Crimes Unit of King County*
*Sheriff's Office, King County, Washington*

Kraske wanted someone who was experienced in serial killing investigations to consult, so he called Bob Keppel, a former homicide detective with the Seattle Police Depart-

ment who had been vital in the investigation of the Ted
Bundy case.

Keppel, who many describe generously as controversial,
believed that when it came to investigating serial killers, tra-
ditional police methods were at the very least ineffective. He
believed in what were considered radical techniques at the
time, such as killer profiling and the perfection of crime
scene investigation. Kraske wanted that type of thinking on
his team of investigators.

He also wanted to establish an open communication policy
between all jurisdictions, including King County, Seattle,
Tacoma, and Kent. The idea was that information would be
shared on each homicide that occurred in each jurisdiction.

Disagreements about who the killer was began to surface
almost immediately. Some detectives thought there was
more than one killer. Others, like Keppel, thought they were
dealing with one killer — a sexual psychopath. The rocks inserted in the victims' vaginas and the tying of their jeans
around the necks of two of the victims were clear indications
to Keppel.

As serial killing investigators know today, dumping bodies
at a particular site is one signature of the killer. During the
Green River killings investigation, FBI experts told the team
that the killer may frequently return to the dumping ground
to not only relive the act, but the site may be a convenient
place for him to send a message.

The task force's next step was to set up a surveillance of
the Green River to see if the killer would make another visit.
In the meantime, Kraske had a police artist sketch the victims whom they couldn't identify, and circulated the draw-
ings in the news media hoping to get some help from the
public.

## An Arrest is Made

The press was demanding answers and Kraske was under pressure. The media was already implying that another serial killer was on the loose in Western Washington.

Detective Larry Gross, whose specialty was finding people who tried to elude the police, found Larry Mathews in a bar that Mathews frequented along the SeaTac Strip. The Strip was a stretch of road that prostitutes walked while picking up tricks. Sleazy bars also populated the Strip — one was the Browne's Star Grill, Mathews' favorite place.

In the early 1980s, the area known as the Strip was a haven for women (mostly young women) working as prostitutes. It was here where a lot of women became victims of the Green River Killer. Prostitution flourished during this time period attracting literally hundreds of young girls looking for "Johns" to make a quick buck.

On August 20, 1982, Gross went to the bar, saw Mathews, and after a fight, arrested Mathews and took him to the King County jail. Under questioning, Mathews denied that he killed anyone, particularly any of the women. There was no physical evidence to connect Mathews to the case, but despite that, Kraske announced to the press that the police had a suspect in custody who was cooperating with the investigation.

When the police searched Mathews' house, they found what they thought was promising evidence. In the basement of the house, the detectives found a pair of handcuffs suspended from the ceiling with chains and what looked like dried blood on them. However, Kraske had jumped the gun, because when the cuffs were tested, the blood didn't match any of the women's blood types, and Mathews was released.

However, on the positive side, after the sketches of the unidentified women ran in the papers, many people came forward to identify the women. After obtaining the dental records, the medical examiner was able to identify the woman that Reichert found as Opal Mills. She was a sixteen-year-old prostitute. The other woman found that day was Cynthia Hinds — her nickname was Cookie. Cookie was well-known to the vice squad because she had a long record for prostitution.

Reichert then proceeded to interview the women's families. His first stop was the family of Opal Mills. He found out that the family had last seen Opal on August 11, when she and her friend Cookie went to work on a temporary job painting apartments. Opal was also trying to get a job for her brother. She called her family around 10:00 p.m. that night and told them she wasn't able to get the job for her brother. They never heard from her again.

Reichert determined that the call had been placed from a phone booth on Pacific Highway South near a motel where victims Deborah Bonner and Marcia Chapman were last seen. According to Reichert, both Mills and Hinds had disappeared one day before Deborah Bonner's body had been found.

When detectives interviewed Cynthia Hinds' family and friends, they discovered that Hinds was last seen at a convenience store on the night that she had disappeared. The store was also only a mile or so from the motel that Deborah Bonner had been near when she disappeared.

Reichert said that during that time, one of the biggest obstacles in the investigation was the prostitutes themselves. They distrusted the police, perhaps fearing that they would be arrested; or because of the fact that a lot of them were runaways, they feared they would be returned home.

"We eventually were able to break down that barrier, but it took a lot to convince the women that we were working on homicides and, at that point, we weren't necessarily concerned about their vice activities," said Reichert.

"Another problem was, I think, that the prostitutes were in a state of denial for so long," said Chief Fae Brooks.

Brooks said another problem was that the police did not know when some of the victims disappeared or if the disappearance was the result of foul play. "The problem with a lot of cases of people missing is that they are missing because they want to be. Many of these girls had left home because they wanted to leave," she said. "A lot of their family members didn't know for a long period of time that some of the girls were missing," she said.

## Victims Continue to Disappear

Gisele Lovvorn's boyfriend told police that she had disappeared from their apartment on July 17. Lovvorn was seventeen when she disappeared, and she was a prostitute, according to her boyfriend. James Tindal said she went to "work" on the Strip that night and he never saw her again. In press accounts, he claimed that police did very little to find his girlfriend, so he started driving up and down the Strip looking for her. Tindal offered a cash reward for information leading to her whereabouts.

Some of the prostitutes had overcome their mistrust and started talking to the police investigators. The detectives learned that Coffield, Mills, Bonner, and Chapman knew each other. Reichert said they often walked the Strip together. He said one theory the police developed was that the killer was a regular customer that the women probably knew.

He said detectives worked the Strip interviewing prostitutes about regular customers, especially those who had displayed violent behavior.

Reichert said several of the women came forward with stories of violent incidents. Most told stories of a man in a truck picking them up, driving them to out-of-the way locations and then being beaten, raped, and threatened with their lives.

## The Blue and White Pickup Truck

A description of a blue and white pickup truck was a recurring clue. One of the first mentions of a blue and white pickup truck came from a young woman who told detectives that she was working the Strip in August when a man in a blue and white pickup truck motioned her over and asked for oral sex. She agreed, and got in the truck. The man hurriedly drove off and produced a gun. He held the gun to her head as he drove down a deserted road. When he stopped the truck, he made her strip and then he raped her. He ushered her back to the truck and asked her if she had heard about the bodies found at Green River. He was heading toward the river. When he pulled up to a stoplight, she pushed the gun away, opened the truck door and ran. She told detectives she didn't report the incident at the time, because she didn't think anything would be done.

Reichert said they then received another report concerning a missing prostitute. That report came from the woman's husband, who was also her pimp. His wife was a sixteen-year-old named Kase Ann Lee.

The next day, police received a report that another prostitute was missing. Terri Milligan was reported missing by her live-in boyfriend. He said Milligan had left the motel where they lived to buy dinner at a nearby fast-food restaurant. She never came home.

With the pattern of the dumping of the bodies at the same location and the close encounters of the prostitutes with the man with the blue and white truck, Kraske decided that the Task Force needed help from the FBI. One of the officers visited the FBI's office in Quantico, Virginia, to talk with John Douglas, an agent who is noted for his concept of profiling criminals and their behavior. Back in the early 1980s, profiling was a new concept that wasn't fully embraced by a lot of police departments.

After examining the evidence that the officer brought with him, Douglas concluded in a written report that the Green River killer chose his victims at random, and by dumping a number of victims at the same site, indicated that he was very familiar with the area. Douglas said the killer took extra time getting rid of the body, which meant he was very comfortable with the area and had no fear of being discovered. That meant he had scouted the area and knew when no one would be around. He also revisited the dumpsite likely to re-live the thrill of the previous killings. Douglas also said in his report that the man may try to stay close to the investigation by contacting the police to offer assistance.

## Another Victim — Another Suspect

In the meantime, Kraske released the information that two more prostitutes were missing (Lee and Milligan).

The police were on the lookout for that blue and white pick-up truck that had surfaced in so many of the prostitutes' stories about violent "Johns." Reichert said that while out on patrol one night, an officer spotted a blue and white pickup

truck and pulled the driver over. The driver was Charles
Clark. A routine background check revealed that Clark
owned two handguns. He was brought in for questioning and
a photograph was taken. When the detectives showed a col-
lage of pictures to some of the prostitutes who had claimed
they were attacked — they identified Clark.

Based on the identification by the women, the police convinced a judge to grant them a search warrant and they proceeded to search Clark's house, looking for any evidence
that may tie him to the murders. Police confiscated anything
that might have been viewed as evidence, such as his clothes
and his guns. Hair and fiber samples were also taken from
Clark's truck.

Clark was then arrested and brought to the police station
for questioning. When asked about the Green River killings,
Clark admitted that he had raped several women but he was
adamant that he never killed any of them or anyone. He took
a polygraph test, and passed. Although Clark was as close to
a suspect that they had come across, Reichert doubted he was
the killer. He was, of course, a kidnapper and rapist, but Reichert said after conducting a thorough investigation it was
discovered that Clark had an alibi for most of the times that
the women were murdered.

"Besides, some of the women he kidnapped and raped
were just left on the road. It didn't seem logical that he
would kill some of the women so violently and not kill the
others," said Reichert. Clark was arrested for kidnapping and
rape.

One of the women who had reported Clark's violent attack
to the police and came in to make an identification of Clark
was a prostitute named Betty Jones. Jones was actually a
woman named Debbie Estes. Estes had run away from home
and her parents had been worried when they contacted the

police and filed a missing persons report. The police had arrested Jones for prostitution on many occasions, but the officers didn't connect her missing person report to her real name. Estes had changed her appearance as well as her name. She dyed her hair, and amazingly, was prostituting and living in a motel with her pimp along Pacific Highway South, right under her parents' nose. Her parents owned a trucking business less than a mile from where their daughter was working the Strip.

After Clark was arrested and placed in jail, Mary Meehan, a young runaway who was staying at a motel with her boyfriend on Pacific Highway South, disappeared after she went out to run a short errand. Meehan wasn't a prostitute and she was eight months pregnant. The killer probably thought she was easy prey because she was walking the Strip alone. When she didn't return to the motel, her boyfriend called the police.

In the meantime, the case was garnering intense media attention. Trying to find some answers, Reichert and one of his partners were following up on John Douglas' profile of the killer. Douglas had told them that the killer would probably want to be involved in the investigation in some way — maybe by donating his time. While many citizens volunteered to help with searches or tedious paperwork, one man in particular attracted their attention. The man was a taxi driver named Melvin Foster.

Reichert said members of the task force initially became suspicious of Foster when he called several times and said he knew a lot about psychology and he knew a lot of the prostitutes that walked the Strip.

When Reichert conducted a background check (which is what the police did on all volunteers on the case) he discovered that Foster had served two prison sentences when he was younger. Reichert invited him in to talk and said he told investigators that likely suspects were other taxi drivers. He even named one man in particular, whose last name was Smith. When police ran a background check on Smith, they discovered he didn't have a police record. When Reichert followed up by questioning Smith, he agreed to a polygraph test and passed.

When Reichert questioned Foster further, he denied having ever used one of the teenage girls as a prostitute. When Reichert confronted him with his prison record, he admitted his jail sentences and explained that he realized that he had made some mistakes. However, he said that he had cleaned up his life and hadn't been in any trouble with the law since 1965.

Reichert wanted to question Foster even further. He set up an interview for the following week of September 20. Foster agreed. After Reichert showed him photographs of the murdered women, he said he knew some of them and their pimps. Reichert carefully proceeded with his questioning. He wanted to know about his relationship with the young women and their pimps. Foster became angry — he thought he was there to help but then he realized he was a suspect. Reichert suggested that he take a polygraph test. After the test was concluded, Reichert told him he didn't pass.

When Reichert asked for permission to search Foster's house, in a move surprising to Reichert, he agreed. Detectives searched the man's house, but didn't come up with any evidence to tie him to the case. Reichert then asked for hair and blood samples and questioned him throughout the night — but Foster didn't change his story. When he wanted to leave, Reichert produced an arrest warrant for parking fines. Foster angrily threatened a huge lawsuit. When he finally left the police station, Reichert placed him under surveillance.

The surveillance continued on a daily basis and after a few weeks, Foster was furious and went to the news media with a story of being followed, questioned for hours, and after co-operating fully with the police, he was still being harassed by them.

The police response to his protest to the media was another more extensive search of his house. The search lasted for more than seven hours — but it didn't reveal any new evidence. After that incident Foster refused to cooperate any further with the police and wouldn't answer any more questions without his lawyer being present. Foster became a sympathetic media figure and had threatened lawsuits if his name was used in the case inappropriately. The police had to back off.

Reichert said an investigation of this kind is very stressful for police officers on many levels. "This guy threatened to kill me on many occasions. He even found out where I lived and sent me the most bizarre, threatening letters that described how he wanted to kill me. I won't go into all the details, but they were really strange," Reichert said.

## More Bodies and More Victims

In the meantime the decomposed body of Gisele Lovvorn was found in late September, 1982. Police positively identified her through her dental records. He nude body had a pair of socks tied around her neck, the same pattern as a couple of the earlier victims.

In addition, another victim was claimed. Denise Bush, a prostitute who lived with her pimp in a motel along Pacific Highway South went out to get something to eat and she never returned. Two days later Shawnda Summers disappeared while she was working that night along the Strip.

By December 10, the ninth victim — an eighteen-year-old prostitute named Rebecca Marrero — disappeared while working the Strip.

By the time that April, 1983, rolled around, more victims had been credited to the Green River killer. Sandra Kay Gabbert worked the Strip and picked up a man — and disappeared.

Then, within hours, Kimi Pastor, a prostitute who was working in downtown Seattle, disappeared. Her pimp told police that he saw a man in a green pickup truck, who signaled that he wanted her services. She got in his truck and was never seen or heard from again. This brought the total to eleven victims.

The detectives were running out of suspects and leads — most of the promising suspects had been cleared through background checks. Ironically, part of the reason for this shortage was that leads were coming in to the task force headquarters at an overwhelming pace. That, coupled with an antiquated computer system, made it virtually impossible to keep track of all the information that was coming in. Reichert, on the advice of Bob Keppel, attempted to organize the investigation.

On top of everything, the killer seemed to be stepping up his pace, because less than two weeks after Gabbert and Pastor disappeared, a pimp reported that Marie Malvar had been picked up on Pacific Highway South by a man in a green pickup truck with a camper. He said he never saw Marie again. However, he waited for more than a week before reporting her disappearance to the police. In an ironic twist, less than a month later, her driver's license was found at a departure gate at SeaTac International airport. When the police ran a check, they discovered that she was one of the missing girls. No one thought to immediately retrieve her license from the airport, therefore eliminating possible clues such as fingerprints. Years later, when the task force tried to locate the driver's license, it had been lost.

On May 3, the police were called out to an area just beyond the Strip, by people who were out on a family hike and found a woman's body. This victim was later identified as Carol Ann Christensen. The killer had apparently changed his MO. She was fully dressed, but there were some unusual twists. There was a paper sack placed over her head, and her body was oddly posed. This victim was easily identifiable. Either the killer was becoming sloppy or he was beginning not to care, because he left her identification in her pocket.

When Reichert checked on the autopsy, the medical examiner told him that the woman had been strangled and that she had been dead approximately twenty-four hours before she was found.

In May, three more victims were found. Martina Authorlee disappeared and was never seen again. Cheryl Wims disappeared two days after, and then, a week later, Yvonne Antosh disappeared. They were all working as prostitutes when they disappeared.

"I remember the killings really started to pick up," said Brooks. "I think by this time, the killer was averaging about two killings a month."

Brooks said it should be noted that some of the women who were killed were not prostitutes. One example, is Constance Naon. In June, 1983, Naon went with friends to happy hour at a bar. Brooks said the twenty-two-year-old was not a prostitute. When she didn't return home that night, her boyfriend became worried and finally reported to the police that she was missing.

Brooks said a couple of days later two more prostitutes turned up missing. First, Tammy Liles disappeared while working in the downtown Seattle area, and Keli Kay McGuiness, who was working the Strip on Pacific Highway South. Bodies continued to be found quite frequently, and like Brooks said, potential victims were being reported missing at least twice a month.

In August, 1983, a man found the skeletal remains of a body on a dirt road near the Strip. When the medical examiner conducted his investigation, he determined that the remains were of a young woman. Her dental records didn't lead to an identification.

In September, the skeletal remains of another young woman were found — almost ten miles from the Strip. Then in October, another woman's remains were found, and this time in an area almost fifteen miles from the Strip. Later that month, another woman's remains were found — another fifteen miles from the Strip. These victims were identified as Shawnda Summers and Yvonne Antosh.

The task force at that time consisted of members from the King County Sheriff's Office, Seattle Police Department, Kent Police Department, and the Pierce County Sheriff's Office, as well as agents from the FBI. Reichert said members of the task force began to become frustrated because they didn't seem to be getting any closer to finding the killer. Despite an exhaustive investigation, the crimes continued with no leads on any new suspects — women were still disappearing and remains were still being found on a regular basis.

Two weeks after the discovery of the remains of Summers and Antosh, two more bodies were found near the airport. One body was buried in a shallow grave. She, too, had a rock inserted in her vagina. The other body was not buried.

"At one point we felt like we were fighting a losing battle because we couldn't convince the prostitutes to curtail their activities," said Brooks. "They kept working as if nothing was happening."

The next prostitute to disappear was eighteen-year-old Paige Miley, who was four months pregnant. Since so many bodies were being found near the airport, the King County Sheriff's Office and the SeaTac Port Police organized a complete search of the area. Volunteers from the Explorer Scouts assisted in the searches. They found the skeletal remains of another body, later identified as that of the pregnant Mary Meehan.

Reichert said that by the end of 1983, the new sheriff decided that more people were needed on the Green River case. The sheriff asked for additional police resources from the county. The sheriff wanted more detectives and a stronger working relationship with the FBI on the case.

The killings were making officials very nervous. After Ted Bundy, no one wanted the Seattle area to become known as the place that produced serial killers. They approved the sheriff's resource request, and John Douglas and a team of FBI agents arrived to work with the detectives.

"It was the first part of January 1984 that we got the new 'enhanced' task force. I think at that point we had sixty-five local investigators, in addition to agents from the FBI," said Reichert.

With the new task force formed, one of its first duties was to develop a way to effectively use and access all the information that detectives had gathered during the lengthy investigation.

With the FBI having so much experience in handling massive investigations, Douglas and the FBI agents were essential in briefing the detectives on how to handle the mammoth amount of information and how to interview suspects. Unfortunately, Douglas' expertise was short-lived to the task force because he became seriously ill and had to leave the area.

Other players were changing as well. Captain Frank Adamson now commanded the task force. The task force was becoming more organized. One of the problems of the previous task force was the inability to coordinate all the information in one central area. The killer was dumping bodies across different city and county lines; unfortunately, each jurisdiction had its own way to conduct an investigation.

Adamson, in an attempt to organize the team, moved the task force to one central headquarters location. He then divided the sixty-five detectives into teams so that they would investigate different aspects of the crime. With these procedures in place, the task force set about a more intensive investigation.

However, it would prove to take more than a reorganization to handle the sheer volume of this case. By February, 1984, the suspect list had grown to more than one thousand names. With that many names, the task force came up with a system to investigate the names on the list. The suspects were arranged into three major categories — with the more likely suspects going into the priority category. The priority category consisted of those men who were known to frequent the Strip and/or who had been violent with women.

## Promising Lead

One lead that the detectives followed up on was an eyewitness account of one of the missing women's pimp. Kimi Pastor's pimp told the detectives that he was with the woman in downtown Seattle when a man in a pickup truck propositioned her.

He gave the police one of the first descriptions of the driver. The pimp described the driver as a big, white man between the ages of twenty to thirty years old with dark curly hair. The police suggested that the man undergo hypnosis so that he could provide a more detailed description. He agreed, and under hypnosis remembered that the man also had a tattoo on his arm, and that his face was scarred from acne. A police sketch was made and circulated.

In the meantime, the task force was still trying to determine exactly how many women were missing, which was difficult without accurate missing persons reports. Reichert said they tried different ways to check. They combed the streets talking with the women, asking if they hadn't seen someone for a while, or they checked court records to see which prostitutes were not showing up for their court dates.

And bodies continued to be found. In February and March of 1984, three more bodies were found. The first two were found near the Cascade Mountains, almost forty-five miles east of downtown Seattle, the opposite direction from where most of the bodies had been found. A month later a second body was found 300 yards from where the body was found in February. This, unfortunately, involved another police district.

Later in March a man found a human bone near the airport. When the task force conducted a search of the area, they discovered the rest of the woman's remains. Since this area was becoming another favorite dumping ground of the killer, the task force organized another search of the area two days later, during which they found another body, or the skeletal remains at least. She was identified as Cheryl Lee Wims.

Then on March 31, 1984, a man out for a walk found bones of another body thirty-five miles outside of downtown Seattle. The same day, another human skull was found off of Star Lake Road.

These were wooded areas and since bodies were being found here, another search was conducted with the help of the Explorer Scouts. It only took two hours for the team of searchers to find two other skeletons. The two victims in this location were identified as Terri Milligan and Sandy Gabbert.

When the search continued the next day, the skeletal remains of another woman were found with the aid of a psychic, who claimed that she had a vision of where the body was. She was in the area where the police were searching. This victim was identified as Amina Agisheff. She was not a prostitute, but a waitress who had disappeared from downtown Seattle. She was last seen on July 7, 1982, when she left work late that night. Agisheff was on her way home to her children and her boyfriend.

The use of different dumping grounds was becoming just as much of a pattern of these killings as the way the women were murdered. Reichert said the task force thought this was a clue to the killer. They tried to determine the pattern by plotting the discoveries on a map. Since the killer had time to hide or bury some of the bodies, the task force concluded that the man knew the areas very well because he knew the comings and goings of traffic in the area. They thought the man either grew up in the area or had lived there for a long period of time. Most of these sites were illegal dumping sites — they thought that also might be a clue to the killer's identity.

In late May another skeleton was found. It was identified through dental records as that of Colleen Brockman, a fifteen-year-old runaway.

As the months passed, new bodies were discovered. In October, 1984, the skeletal remains of Mary Sue Bello were found. A month later, authorities found the remains of Martina Authorlee.

Reichert said that by late 1984 and early 1985, the task force had compiled more than 10,000 pieces of physical evidence. Each piece of evidence had to go through a scientific examination by the state crime lab. However, the lab was hampered by the lack of computers to quickly log information, or in the case of fingerprints, to run matches by computers instead of by manual comparison.

The state lab's inability to provide a quick turnaround of information became a target of criticism from within the task force. In order to eliminate suspects from their lists or concentrate fully on one suspect, they needed the evidence.

In March, another body was found near Star Lake Road. She was a fifteen-year-old named Carrie Rois.

The profilers on the case had told the task force that it was possible that the killer, feeling the detectives might be getting close to apprehending him, could move to a different city to continue his killing spree. Reichert said that by comparing similar crimes in surrounding areas, it was determined that strange disappearances of prostitutes were happening in these places as well, one of those places being Portland, Oregon.

He said Portland authorities were contacted, and at first they were reluctant to believe that the killer had moved to or was operating in their city. However, in June, 1985, when a bulldozer driver doing some excavation work discovered several skeletons, they changed their minds. One of the skulls was examined and identified as Denise Bush, who had disappeared from the Strip in 1982.

"Part of her remains were found in Portland and part of her remains were found in Seattle," said Reichert. "So something unusual definitely was going on. Either the killer was murdering the women here, waiting for the bodies to decompose and then transporting the bodies there, or vice-versa."

Brooks said that since the killer had crossed state lines, the FBI had primary investigative authority at that point. The FBI and members of the Green River task force went to Portland to conduct an investigation and they conducted another search of the area.

They found more bones, and were informed that the skeletal remains of two women were found in a nearby town. One of those women was identified as nineteen-year-old prostitute named Shirley Sherill. She was last seen working the Strip in 1982.

## Was There More Than One Killer?

Since so many areas and now a different state were involved, the inevitable question arose of whether there was more than one killer, or maybe a copycat killer.

Reichert said he believed then and still believes that there was one killer in the Green River case. However, he said that FBI profiler John Douglas prepared a report that stated there was a possibility that there was more than one killer.

The Douglas report compared how the bodies dumped at the Green River were relatively fresh and out in the open — indicating that the killer wanted them to be found, as opposed to most of the victims that weren't found at the river;

in those cases the killer had tried to hide the bodies, since most were decomposed when found.

"We not only relied on John Douglas and the FBI, but we worked with profilers here in the Seattle area, such as forensic psychiatrists and forensic dentists," said Reichert.

The police were also in the process of identifying some of the other victims — Lisa Yates and Delores Williams were two of the victims that were identified.

"I think it's hard for most people to understand how difficult investigating these crimes were. The fact that the murders were stranger to stranger made it difficult to backtrack the victims' last contacts," said Reichert. "Also, the killer was usually three or four months ahead of us and the bodies, in a lot of cases, were decomposed. I remember after we discovered the first few bodies, Bob Keppel, who had worked on the Ted Bundy case and was one of the detectives who worked on the Wayne Williams Atlanta children's case, as well as others, telling me, 'you are going to have a lot more bodies' — and they were right."

## So Much Evidence

Reichert said one of the positives in the case was the introduction of VICAP (Violent Criminal Apprehension Program). Reichert and the task force worked with a retired detective from the Los Angeles Police Department, who was one of the first officers to utilize the system.

VICAP, in theory, allowed police departments across the country to log information about unsolved murders in a central computer system so they could track similar crimes in different areas or different states. In actuality, not many departments used the system, therefore making it a less effective investigative tool.

Pierce Brooks, the Los Angeles detective, advised that even more resources be devoted to the Green River task force because everything had to be meticulously checked. Brooks, who was very experienced at working on multiple homicides, gave the task force his own profile of the killer. Reichert said he agreed with a lot of what Brooks said, such as that the killer probably worked alone. And, that since he struck at different times and in different areas, he probably worked part-time or had a very flexible work schedule, or was maybe even a member of the military.

In addition, Brooks had said that the killer probably had selected the dumpsites prior to killing his victims. He suggested that the task force create their own leads and try to check both every detail of the victims' lives, and people who fit any of the descriptions that prostitutes had given of men with which they had violent encounters.

"We collected every list you could think of, including checking out everybody who had a green pickup truck, cab drivers, and, since some of the women were found in the river with steelhead trout, we checked out people with fishing licenses," said Reichert.

Almost from the beginning of the discovery of the bodies, the news media was very critical of the investigation.

"I think their impression was, 'what's taking so long?' or that we (the police) weren't too concerned about the crimes because most of the women were prostitutes," said Reichert. "The public or the media didn't understand that we were doing everything we could. I know for a fact that people who worked on the case gave it their all. They willingly worked nights and weekends. To have the news media criticize us so

---

unmercifully was hard to take — but at least the families knew we cared."

By the end of December, 1985, another human skull was found near a wrecked car on Star Lake Road. After police made a search of the area the next day, they found the rest of the woman's remains. The police resumed the search of the area a few days later and found another skull. Based on those discoveries, police combed the area and found other skeletal remains belonging to Kimi Pastor. There was no identification of the other two bodies.

## Another Arrest

On February 6, 1986, the task force, along with the FBI, made a dramatic arrest. They arrested a man named Ernest McLean, whose house was located just off the Strip. Officers descended upon the house with a search warrant and removed boxes of "evidence." With the press carefully watching and clamoring for information, then-Detective Fae Brooks, who was Media Relations Officer, made the announcement, reluctantly, that the task force was detaining a "person of interest."

MacLean was questioned for hours, surrounded by pictures of the women. "We knew we had to be careful in how we questioned him. On the advice of the profiler we set up the room that way," said Reichert. "We confronted him with the evidence, but eventually, it became apparent that he wasn't the killer."

When Brooks made the announcement that MacLean was being released, the press had a field day. Both Seattle papers relentlessly criticized the entire investigation, accusing the task force of being inept. Of course, even though Brooks had described MacLean as a "person of interest," the papers had described him as a suspect — even going as far as printing his name.

"That was really hard," said Reichert. "An investigation of that kind is very complex. We had hundreds of suspects that we had to follow up on and question." To further complicate an already complicated investigation, members of the FBI decided to leave the task force and return to their normal duties, and some members of the task force left the team or were reassigned. Reichert, who had been on the investigation from the very start of the killings, witnessed the changes. "It was not only members of the press or the community who were impatient, it was some of the members of the task force. Some would come in with the attitude that we're going to wrap this up in six months. And when that didn't happen, a lot of the detectives would say, "I can't handle this," and they left," Reichert recalls. "I think a lot of people really underestimated the stress and the enormity of investigating a serial killing."

In the meantime, three more victims' remains were found. Two of the victims were discovered in Seattle; they were identified as Maureen Feeney and Kim Nelson, two more prostitutes. The third was found along the Green River. She was not immediately identified. During that time, a county review committee decided to cut the task force substantially. "At its largest we had more than sixty-five investigators plus agents from the FBI. We saw a slow, steady cutback of resources," said Reichert.

"The cuts couldn't have come at a worse time. We had more than 10,000 pieces of evidence to catalog and evaluate, as well as more than 40,000 tips to follow up on," said Reichert. "We also still had hundreds of suspects to interview and conduct background checks on."

By 1986, the killings appeared to have stopped. In case the killer had moved to another area because he was under scrutiny in the Seattle area, the detectives paid particular attention to similar crimes in other areas.

In December, 1989, two victims were found in Vancouver, in the British Columbia province of Canada. Vancouver is a 3.5-hour drive from Seattle, so it was plausible that the killer could still be in the area and took drives up to Canada. Reichert found out that the women worked in a club as topless dancers.

In June, 1987, three boys found the skeletal remains of another body. She was identified as Cindy Ann Smith, a topless dancer who had disappeared in January, 1984, while hitchhiking along the Strip.

In September, another body was found. She was identified as a sixteen-year-old runaway prostitute named Rose Marie Kurran. Her body had not decomposed indicating that it was a recent homicide. The police assumption that the killings had stopped wasn't necessarily true. A few days later another partially decomposed body was found in the Black Diamond area. She was identified as fourteen-year-old Debbie Ann Gonzales.

By 1988, the task force was a shell of its former self, and was under the threat of its resources being cut even further. A lot of the detectives had been reassigned.

In May, 1988, a construction crew found some human bones. Through dental record identification, the woman was identified as Debbie Estes, who had disappeared in 1982. Earlier that month another identification was made. Tammy Liles was sixteen years old when she was murdered in 1985. Her body had been found in Oregon.

It had been a while since the task force had received any reports of recent missing women. The task force kept monitoring similar crimes occurring in different parts of the country. One city that was having similar crimes, prostitutes being murdered and their bodies being dumped, was San Diego, California.

The killings had dated back to 1984, and Reichert went to San Diego to find if there were any connections between the their crimes and the Green River Killer.

"I worked with Detective Craig Henderson," said Reichert. "Prostitutes were being killed and then dumped in the same area. Detective Henderson and I reviewed each case individually, and even though they were similar, we determined that it was a different killer. I think it was proved that San Diego had two or three separate killers operating," said Reichert.

By 1988, the task force needed a fresh approach. In December, they hoped that a television program about the killings would result in new leads on the case. On December 7, 1988, Crime Stoppers sponsored a program on the killings hosted by Patrick Duffy of the *Dallas* television program fame. The studio was equipped with phone lines and operators (mostly detectives) to take information. They answered more than 15,000 calls during the program.

Reichert said that a lot of the leads weren't useful, but the rest were entered in the task force computer and compared against the information they had already collected.

"As you can imagine, it was an enormous task. We also got a lot of confessions that had to be checked out. Some of the confessions we could immediately dismiss, but some we had to take seriously," said Reichert.

## Another Suspect

One of the calls tipped the detectives off to another possible suspect. His name was William J. Stevens. Stevens had been sentenced to a prison term on a burglary charge, but had escaped in 1981. Apparently he had been living in the Spokane, Washington, area for a number of years (he had attended law school at Gonzaga University from 1985-1988 *á la* Ted Bundy) and he fit the killer's profile on many levels. He had served in the U.S. Army, and after he finished his duty he had tried to become a police officer by applying to the Seattle Police Department. His application was denied.

"Stevens was quite interesting," said Reichert. "He was definitely into collecting police memorabilia. During the search of his house, we found that he had a police uniform, what looked like a badge, and I think he even had a police car."

When the task force conducted a background investigation of Stevens' whereabouts and activities since 1982, they found out quite a bit about him. When they talked to people who knew him, they were told that Stevens had an unusual interest or maybe even a preoccupation with the Green River killings, and that he often expressed his hatred of prostitutes. Stevens frequently made visits to the Seattle, Portland, and Vancouver areas.

He also owned a house near Portland in Tigard, Oregon, investigators said.

When they thought they had enough to move on, the police arrested Stevens on the old escape charge. When they searched his home, they found several unregistered weapons, fake identification, credit cards with different names, and boxes of sexual photographs of nude prostitutes. "He had secret compartments to rooms in his house — it was very strange," said Reichert. Stevens was returned to prison to serve his sentence on the escape charge, while detectives tried to build a case against him on the Green River killings.

Stevens had a good reputation in law school. However, acquaintances said that he often gave the impression that he was part of the Green River Task Force in an official capacity. When members of the task force attempted to question Stevens, he refused to cooperate and directed all their questions to his attorney.

When the contents of the search of Stevens' house were examined, the task force couldn't connect any of it to the murders. They then acquired a search warrant for Stevens' parents' home and a storage unit that he had rented in Spokane with the same results. So, the announcement had to be made that Stevens was no longer a suspect.

"We were able eliminate him from being the killer in many of the women's deaths," said Reichert. The police added illegal firearm charges against Stevens. He died of cancer shortly after he left prison.

The total number of women killed by the Green River killer was officially listed at forty-nine — although Sheriff Reichert admits the number could be higher.

# Reflections on
# the Green River Case

Sheriff Reichert worked on the Green River case from its beginning in 1982 until the task force was disbanded in 1990. Even though he and other detectives on the case have moved on in their careers, thoughts of the case still linger for them. He talked to me about his reflections on the case.

"The investigation was hard, it was stressful, and it was emotional — but it's important to remember that we did some good things. We solved a number of rapes and robberies," he said. "We actually solved two other serial killings and found more than 2000 reportedly missing women."

The case also took a personal toll on Reichert. "I worked the case almost exclusively for eight years, and believe me, I paid a personal price. During the first four years I was absolutely obsessed with finding the killer. I was away from home a lot, and even when I went to family functions I would sit off by myself, thinking about the case and wondering what have we done — what have we missed — who I should interview or re-interview."

Reichert said his children were growing up and he needed to come to terms with working the case. "The last four years, I learned to achieve more of a balance," he said.

One of the factors that contributed to the stress, according to Reichert, was the public's perception that the police weren't working as hard as they could to solve the case. "I remember at one point, a group of women had a "Take Back the Night" sit-in at the courthouse. I just remember buying boxes of doughnuts and hot chocolate and going to sit among them — to let them know I was just as concerned about the killings as they were," he said.

Serial killings are hard to solve, and the Green River case was no exception. Reichert said that one of the problems is that prostitutes usually make easy prey for this kind of killer. "It usually takes a while to realize that they are missing, and it's even harder to establish who they were last seen with," he said.

The fact that most of the women were so young was also a source of sadness. "You know cops don't just focus on the crime — we just can't separate ourselves from our human part," said Reichert. "It was sad that a majority of the girls were so young. But from talking to most of them, there was nothing but pain for them at home. So, amazingly, the street and prostitution was for them, in many ways, preferable."

Reichert spent a great deal of time traveling to compare similar crimes from other areas of the country. His travels even took him to Florida's State Penitentiary death row to talk with condemned serial killer Ted Bundy.

"Bob Keppel and I went down there to interview him. He had written Bob offering his help. I know he did it out of purely selfish reasons, most likely to try to delay his execution as long as possible. But I thought it was good to interview him because it gave me a good idea of what our guy would be like," Reichert explained.

He said Bundy told them some of the factors that contributed to the killer eluding the police. Among them were that the victims he chose (prostitutes) were readily accessible, they were transient and, therefore, their disappearance wouldn't be immediately noticed. And since these women came and went many times during the night, it would be hard to trace their paths.

Reichert had to agree with most of what he told them. He said tracing the women's movements was a very difficult part of the investigation. "We were dealing with witnesses who were not the most reliable people. The prostitutes themselves saw a lot of people on a daily basis, so there was a lot of confusion as to what day or week they last saw one of the missing girls."

He said Bundy also told them that the killer had probably stalked most of his victims enough to know their habits, and that the killer probably was known to the girls — but probably not as a customer.

Reichert believes there was only one killer operating in the Green River killings — unlike cases in Los Angeles or San Diego. "The San Diego case, as an example, had twenty-five or thirty prostitute killings — it was eventually proved to be two or three separate killers."

And Reichert said that even though they had many suspects that didn't pan out to be the Green River killer, some of them were arrested for other crimes. According to a newspaper article, one of those suspects, John Hanks, was linked to the deaths of six women in California. The women were strangled and their bodies dumped. Hanks had a history of violence against women. In fact, he was convicted in 1967 of killing his sister-in-law.

Fae Brooks, who is now Chief of the Major Crimes Unit in the King County Sheriff's Office, said she's still committed to solving the case even after all these years. "From my perspective, someone will always be working on the case until it is solved," Brooks said. Toward that commitment, Brooks still keeps a sheet of paper listing all the names of the victims, the dates they were missing, and the dates their bodies were recovered. "While looking at some of these names, I can still see some of their faces," Brooks said. "I knew some of the girls from previous arrests for prostitution. One of the girls, Martha Chapman, was a rape victim about six months before she died. I got the opportunity to know her very well and it was really hard when she was found murdered."

Brooks said she hopes that with the technological advances occurring today, some DNA evidence will surface that will enable them to find the killer.

"My dream is that someday we will get a phone call from a caretaker at one of those storage facilities and they complain that someone hasn't paid their bill and they are throwing away the contents in the unit. When we get there we find definitive evidence of the killings and it's backed up by DNA," she said.

Of course, that's a dream, but in the meantime Detective Tom Jenkins is the only detective still working full-time on the case. In updating me on the case, he said he still spends a great deal of time following up on tips that the case still generates. "I still receive calls from people who think they know who the Green River killer is," he said.

Jenkins is a veteran of the case, having joined the Green River task force back in 1984. "The murders were winding down when I joined the task force, but that was not known for several years," he said. He said that he's determined to identify all the young women. Four victims still remain unidentified.

I asked him if when he hears about the same kind of killings in different parts of the country, does he think the killer has simply moved on?

"You know, the trouble with the Green River killings is that they were pretty generic. All over this country, a prostitute is strangled and killed on any given day," said Jenkins. He said the uniqueness of this case was the number of women who were killed, the frequency at which they were killed, and how the bodies were dumped.

Brooks said some good came from the investigation, in that the King County police changed some of their procedures. "We definitely act more quickly on missing persons cases now — and we ask immediately for dental records and log them in the National Crime Information Center (NCIC)," she said. "I think it made me a more compassionate officer, and it made our department better in perfecting crime scene investigations and techniques. A lot of what we had to do in the Green River case was to get on our hands and knees and search for any scrap of evidence. We're certainly a lot better

---

at that, and we recognize what is evidence a lot more quickly."

Brooks' dedication to the case lives on. One of the women, Tracy Winston, missing since 1983, was found in March, 1986. Winston was officially identified in the year 2000 by DNA testing. Both Brooks and Reichert attended the funeral.

# Selected Bibliography

There were numerous other newspapers articles and police reports that contributed to the research of this book.

## Television Programs and Videos

A&E *Biography — Eliot Ness: Untouchable.*

A&E *Biography — George Reeves*, February, 2000.

A&E *Biography — Bob Crane: A Double Life,* February, 2000.

A&E *City Confidential — Old Hollywood: Silent Stars Deadly Secrets*, March 2000.

A&E *City Confidential : Skidmore — Frontier Justice.*

Court TV — *Roscoe "Fatty" Arbuckle.*

MSNBC *Crime Files — Bob Crane.*

History Channel — *History's Mysteries: Vanished (Judge Crater and other famous disappearances).*

History Channel — *True Story of the Untouchables.*

History Channel — *William Desmond Taylor*, April 2000.

*Hoffa* (Jack Nicholson) VHS Video.

# Periodicals

"Two Missing Women Fit Profile of Green River Killer Victims," *Seattle Times*, September 29, 1982.

"250 Questioned in Green River Probe," *Seattle Times*, September 9, 1982.

"Third Murder Victim Found in Green River is Identified," *Seattle Times*, August 18, 1982.

"Seven-Hour Search: Police Comb Home of Green River Suspect," *Seattle Times*, November 23, 1982.

"A Body is Found in Green River Area (along Auburn-Black Diamond Road)," *Seattle Times*, September 27, 1987.

"All Five women Slain Linked to Prostitution," *Seattle Times*, August 25, 1982.

Barron, James, "60 Years Ago Tonight, Judge Crater Stepped Into a Taxi," *New York Times*, August 6, 1990.

"Bodies Found in River Make Total of Twelve Similar Cases," *Seattle Times,* August 17, 1982.

Bradsley, Marilyn, *Eliot Ness: The Man Behind the Myth,* (Internet Access)

"Cabbie Says He's Suspect in Murders," *Seattle Times*, October 5, 1982.

"Cops Say Green River Killer May Kill Again," *Seattle Post Intelligencer,* September 2, 1982.

"Discovery of Skeleton Prompts Search (near airport)," *Seattle Times*, November 1, 1983.

"FBI Enters Missouri Shooting Case," *New York Times*, July 1, 1981.

"FBI Profile Says Killer May Return to Crime Scene," *Seattle Times*, October 8, 1982.

"Green River Probers Hunger for Arrest," *Seattle Post Intelligencer,* March 24, 1984.

"Green River Slayings Case Becomes a Watch-and-Wait Operation," *Seattle Times*, November 19, 1982.

"Green River Suspect Implicated in Deaths of Two California Women," *Seattle Times*, October 19, 1982.

"Green River Suspect Linked to Six California Killings," *Seattle Times*, October 21, 1982.

"It's 1974 All Over Again to the Cops Leading Probe of Green River Murders (Richard Kraske)," *Seattle Post Intelligencer*, *October* 3, 1982.

Jones, Robert, *Tales from the Dark Side of Hollywood*, Los Angeles, August 21, 1996.

"Key Clue to Green River Murders is Missing a Year Later," *Seattle Times*, July 16, 1983.

Margolick, David, "Sixty-three Years After his Disappearance, the Search for Judge Crater Continues," *New York Times*, August 6, 1993.

"Medical Examiner Says Renton Woman Strangled," *Seattle Post Intelligencer*, May 9, 1984.

"Murder Victims — Roving Prostitutes or 'Just Missing'," *Seattle Times*, November 20, 1983.

"Murders: 'Girls Just Walking to their Fate'," *Seattle Times*, July 21, 1983.

*Newsweek,* August 1975, "The Hoffa Case."

"No One Is Indicted in Death of 'Bully'," *New York Times*, September 26, 1981.

Peterson, Iver, "Missouri Town Is Silent Over Shooting of the County Bully," *New York Times*, July 17, 1981.

"Police Double Task Force in Bid to Solve Green River Murders," *Seattle Post Intelligencer*, November 22, 1983.

"Police Widen Scope of Green River Probe," *Seattle Times*, December 30, 1983.

Schuyler Ingle, "Death Stalks the Street Walker," *The Weekly*, January 25, 1984.

"Serial Killers: Murders Without Motive Confound Police," *Seattle Times*, November 26, 1983.

"Slain Woman Was Running Scared in Final Days," *Seattle Times*, August 18, 1982

"Suspect Arrested in Green River Slayings," *Seattle Times*, August 21, 1982.

"Suspect No Longer Under Surveillance," *Seattle Times*, November 24, 1982.

"The Hoffa Files," *Detroit Sunday Journal*, July and August 1997.

"Theater-Loving Policeman Leads Search for a Killer (Frank Adamson)," *Seattle Times*, February 12, 1984.

"Three Slain Women Found in River Remain Unidentified," *Seattle Times*, August 17, 1982.

"Waitress Who Was Strangled Disappeared Mysteriously," *Seattle Post Intelligencer*, May 11, 1983.

## Books

Barlow, John Martin, *Butcher's Dozen*, New York, 1950.

John Canning, ed., *Great Unsolved Mysteries,* Chartwell Books, New Jersey, 1984.

Collins, Max Allan, *Butcher's Dozen*, New York: Bantam, 1988.

Fraley, Oscar, *Four Against the Mob*, New York: Award Books, 1976.

Graysmith, Robert, *The Murder of Bob Crane*, Berkley Publishing Group, July 1994.

Heimel, Paul, *Eliot Ness: The Real Story*, Knox Books.

Hoffa, James R., as told to Oscar Fraley, *Hoffa: The Real Story,* New York: Stein and Day, 1975.

Kashner, Sam, and Schoenberger, Nancy, *Hollywood Kryptonite: The Bulldog, The Lady,* and *the Death of Superman*, St. Martin's Press, 1996.

Keppel, Robert D., Ph.D., with Birnes, William, J., *The Riverman — Ted Bundy and I Hunt for the Green River Killer,* Pocket Books, New York, 1995.

Kirkpatrick, Sidney D., *A Cast of Killers,* New York: E.P. Dutton, 1986.

Lancaster, Bob — Hall, B.C., *Judgment Day,* Putnam, New York, 1983.

MacLean, Harry, *In Broad Daylight: A Murder In Skidmore, Missouri,* New York: Dell, 1988.

Nickel, Steven, *Torso: The Story of Eliot Ness and the Search for a Psychopathic Killer*, John F. Blair, 1989

Sheridan, Walter, *The Fall and Rise of Jimmy Hoffa*, Saturday Review Press, 1972.

Sifakis, Carl, *The Encyclopedia of American Crime,* New York, 1982.

Sloane, Arthur, A. *Hoffa,* MIT Press, July, 1992.

Smith, Carlton, and Guillen, Thomas, *The Search for the Green River Killer,* Onyx/Penguin Books, New York, 1991.

## Web sites

www.Hoffafiles.com

www.Hoffa.com

www.angelfire.com/ az/Taylorology

www.Hogan'sHeroes.com

# YOU WILL ALSO WANT TO READ:

☐ **34070    BAD GIRLS DO IT!, An Encyclopedia of Female Murderers, *by Michael Newton.*** From the author of *Hunting Humans* and *Killer Cops* comes the *only* book on female multiple murderers ever assembled. Over 180 necrophilic nurses, baby butchers, black widows and angels of death are chillingly catalogued in this grisly collection. Each blood-thirsty babe is described in detail, including childhood experiences, early crimes, how they killed and how they were caught. Based on  ten years of research, ***Bad Girls Do It!*** proves that the urge to kill is an equal opportunity affliction. *1993, 8½ x 11, 205 pp, soft cover.* **$16.95.**

☐ **34084  KILLER COPS, An Encyclopedia of Lawless Lawmen, *by Michael Newton.*** In America, citizens are killed by the police every day of the year, and we have come to expect it. But over the years a few sworn protectors of the law have used their badges as hunting licenses, killing on a whim for profit, sex, or personal revenge. The cases profiled in this book span the continent and run the gamut of law enforcement's social scale, from small-town police departments to the normally sacrosanct FBI, from the Old West's legendary Wyatt Earp to today's bad lieutenants. *1997, 5½ x 8½, 232 pp, soft cover.* **$14.95.**

☐ **34086  HOLY HOMICIDE, An Encyclopedia of Thos Who Go With *Their* God... and Kill!, *by Michael Newton.*** This is a grisly lexicon of murders, which the perpetrators attributed to divine instruction. Murder for religious reasons is the backbone of human history, and the author catalogues this phenomenon by including entries for cults, historical overviews, organized religions and groups, and scores of individuals from all walks of life. *1998, 5½ x 8½, 286 pp, soft cover.* **$16.95.**

# YOU WILL ALSO WANT TO READ:

☐ **34088 COP KILLERS, An Encyclopedia, *by Michael Newton.*** Cops. Some people love them. Some people hate them. Some people kill them. Michael Newton, master of the crime encyclopedia, has compiled more than 100 cases in which legendary gangs, religious mercenaries, and reckless outlaws have taken out law enforcers. You'll meet Bonnie and Clyde, merciless *Mafiosi*, the teenager who claimed rap made him do it, and others in a close look at the tragic way some cops ended their careers. *1998, 5½ x 8½, 346 pp, soft cover.* **$16.95**.

☐ **34092 BLACK COLLAR CRIMES, An Encyclopedia of False Prophets and Unholy Orders, *by Michael Newton.*** What's up with the clergy? Some of these supposedly God-fearing folks are flouting the law of the land. Murder, rape, kidnapping, torture, conspiracy, slavery, prostitution, forgery and lots more. Michael Newton has catalogued a grim host of decidedly un-saintly characters in this book. This lexicon of lawless-ness is truly astounding! You'll never view the clergy in the same way you do now, once you've read Newton's amazing expose of religious misconduct! Read *Black Collar Crimes* now, and prepare yourself for a harsh blast of secular reality. *1998, 5½ x 8½, 280p, soft cover.* **$18.95**.

☐ **34093 STILL AT LARGE, A Casebook of 20th Century Serial Killers Who Eluded Justice, *by Michael Newton.*** They get away with murder. Every year in America, more than 5,000 killers elude police. And most of the notorious murderers who slip the grip of the law commit the same crime again and again, leaving the grisliest of signatures. Michael Newton, master of the crime ency-clopedia, recounts chilling tales of unsolved serial mur-ders. *1998, 5½ x 8½, 328 pp, soft cover.* **$16.95**.

*We offer the very finest in controversial and unusual books? —
A complete catalog is sent FREE with every book order. If you
would like to order the catalog separately, please see our ad on
the last page of this book.*

**Please send me the books I have marked below:**

- ❑ 34070, Bad Girls Do It!, $16.95
- ❑ 34084, Killer Cops, $14.95
- ❑ 34086, Holy Homicide, $16.95
- ❑ 34088, Cop Killers, $16.96
- ❑ 34092, Black Collar Crime, $16.95
- ❑ 34092, Still at Large, $16.95

---

BMM2

**LOOMPANICS UNLIMITED
PO BOX 1197
PORT TOWNSEND, WA 98368**

I am enclosing $ _____ which includes $5.95 for
shipping and handling of orders up to $25.00. Add $1.00 for
each additional $25.00 ordered. *Washington residents
please include 8.3% for sales tax.*

NAME _____

ADDRESS _____

CITY _____

STATE/ZIP _____

We accept Visa, Discover, and MasterCard.
To place a credit card order *only,* call 1-800-380-2230
24 hours a day, 7 days a week.

Check out our Web site: www.loompanics.com